THE WORLD OF THE WASP

THE WORLD
OF THE WASP

Joy O. I. Spoczynska

FRES, FZS, FBIS

Illustrated by Melchior Spoczynski

CRANE, RUSSAK & COMPANY, INC.
NEW YORK

Published in the United States by
Crane, Russak & Company, Inc.
347 Madison Avenue
New York, N.Y. 10017

Copyright © 1975 Joy O. I. Spoczynska, FRES, FZS, FBIS
Photographs © 1975 George E. Hyde, FRES

ISBN 0–8448–0560–2
Library of Congress Catalog Card No 74–13621

Printed in Great Britain

For
DHANJI

Acknowledgements

SO many people have contributed to the making of this book that it is difficult to know where to start in acknowledging my grateful thanks.

I must mention with gratitude the various helpers who assisted me when collecting in West Africa, Guyana, India and the southern United States—not only with the actual collecting but also with the more mundane but equally vital work involved in setting up camp in the jungle and travelling many hundreds of miles, often under very trying climatic conditions and without any mechanised transport.

I must record my grateful thanks to Dr. Paul Freeman, Keeper of Entomology at the British Museum (Natural History) and his staff, who afforded me every facility for research in the Department and, in particular, to my son Melchior Spoczynski who has so ably contributed the line illustrations to this book. I am indebted to him for giving up so much of his free time to collaborate with me in the preparation of this book by doing all the drawings.

My two long-suffering secretaries must not be overlooked – Nina Ikpeme and Bahadur Banerji, both of whom took upon themselves a great deal of the basic work of typing the preliminary drafts, and whose unfailing humour sustained me at those times, common to all authors, when the volume of work involved threatened to overshadow the original enthusiasm.

Finally, I should like to acknowledge the assistance of A. E. Gardiner, Curator of the British Entomological and Natural History Society, for the loan of specimens from their collection, and to S. A. Williams, the Society's Librarian, for the loan of papers and separata for reference.

J.O.I.S.

London, September 1973

Contents

List of Illustrations

Halftone illustrations between pages 96 and 97

Line drawings

CHAPTER I

Introducing Wasps

My first introduction to wasps was in 1959, when I was on a field trip in the Norfolk Broads studying and collecting fenland moths. I had just come in from a particularly hot and exhausting walk, to find wasps busy at the setting-boards of moths which I had caught and set the previous night and propped up on the window-ledge to dry in a current of air. Wasps were making short work of the bodies of my choicest specimens, leaving nothing but a litter of detached wings and legs. These particular wasps are defined as social insects, as we shall see presently—but I need hardly say that I was feeling distinctly anti-social towards them at that time!

Soon afterwards it struck me rather forcibly that set moths' bodies were not the usual food of wasps. After all, the number of people in Britain who set moths and prop up the boards on the window-ledge must form an infinitesimal proportion of the population. I had always thought of wasps in connection with over-ripe fruit, or getting into the jam at picnics; why, then, this apparent departure from the norm? Being more than a little intrigued, I intended to find out; and so began my exploration into the fascinating world of the wasp—a world at that time completely unknown to me.

The exploration has led me into some of the most fascinating places in the world—from the jungles of West Africa to the swamps of Georgia and the Everglades of Florida; from Guyana, land of many waters, where the only way to travel is hundreds of miles by canoe, to dried-up river-beds in a practically waterless region of India, where collecting conditions were the most difficult I have ever experienced. My explorations have taken me from busy suburban localities with traffic roaring past only yards away, to what must be one of the last remaining uninhabited regions left on earth, in which I was, to my knowledge, the first human being ever to set foot.

My favourite collecting-grounds in Britain have also provided me with a very rich harvest of study material—indeed, I was exploring these long before I ever set foot in the tropics.

To many people—perhaps the majority—the word 'wasp' conjures up a fierce buzzing creature, clad in belligerent yellow-and-black stripes, and wielding a deadly sting. They see it as a menace to the jam-making housewife, a fearsome danger to the family on summer picnics and generally an aggressive beast only too ready to attack the unsuspecting human with its sting, and to be 'swatted' at all costs with the nearest available weapon.

Nothing could be further from the truth. A wasp stings only in self-defence, or to paralyse or kill the small insects and spiders which it feeds to its young. In the former case, it will sting only if someone or something is actively interfering with it. After all, wouldn't *you* try to K.O. a burglar in your house in the middle of the night? If a thoughtless person annoys your normally placid dog, he will snap. But if your dog is left in peace, he will not behave in this way; neither will you react aggressively if no intruder threatens the quiet enjoyment of your home. Similarly, if wasps are simply ignored as they go about their business, they will make no attempt to sting; only if actively disturbed will they defend themselves, which is hardly unreasonable. Only the females sting, anyway, but among the social wasps the females greatly outnumber the males, the 'workers' being in fact sterile females, but their stinging ability is unimpaired.

But, you may say, the housewife does not want wasps settling on the jam. True, no one wants them to, but at least you do not have to throw away the jam if they do. Unlike flies, which habitually walk on filth, breeding in dung, rotting meat, dustbins and so on, wasps are much more fastidious in their habits and confine their attentions to fruit and other innocuous materials. As we shall see, the social nest-builders even employ workers for the sole purpose of cleaning out the nest and dumping the waste materials at a considerable distance from it!

Not all wasps are social insects, however; many are solitary, and a good proportion are parasitic. Almost all the non-parasitic species are active predators, whether social or otherwise, catching other insects and spiders to feed their young, although the adults themselves feed only on fruit juices and nectar. Both these and the parasitic wasps are friends of the gardener, destroying vast quantities of harmful aphids, beetle and sawfly grubs as well as the larvae of the cabbage white butterfly, the turnip moth and other pests of crops. In return the horticulturist ought not to begrudge the wasps their sweet spoils from the autumn fruits as a return for their labours, especially since in nine cases out of ten the fruit is already overripe or damaged before the wasps will partake of it.

The Hymenoptera ('membrane-winged' insects), which include not only wasps but bees, ants, ichneumons, chalcids, braconids and gall-wasps as well as the sawflies and horntails, are the third largest order of insects on earth. First come the Coleoptera or beetles, which boast about 275,000 different known species throughout the world; second only to them are the Lepidoptera (butterflies and moths) with about 200,000, while the number of known Hymenoptera, in third world place, drops rather dramatically to 100,000. But 100,000 is still a lot of Hymenoptera—of which the wasps form by far the great majority.

Many more new species certainly await discovery, even in Britain, which has only about 6,100 known species—just over sixteen per cent of the world total. A percentage of nearly one-fifth of the world total is not bad for a tiny island when compared with the rest of the world.

In Britain the Hymenoptera are the largest group, the number of species being nearly double those of the beetles and nearly three times the number of butterflies and moths. New beetles and moths are being discovered in Britain almost every year, some of them of quite ample proportions; how much more likely is it, therefore, that several of the smaller wasps, for example chalcids and gall-wasps under two or three millimetres in length, are busily going about their daily lives unknown even to the eagle-eyed hymenopterists who are out collecting! *You* might easily be the next person to spot a species of wasp new to Britain, or even new to science.

The statistics for the various groups of the British Hymenoptera are given below in tabular form:

SUB-ORDER APOCRITA

Sub-group Aculeata		*No. of species*
Social wasps:	Hornet	1
	Others	6
Solitary wasps:	Potters and masons	15
	Spider-hunters	38
	Cuckoo-wasps or ruby-tails	21
	Fossorial wasps	103
	Mutillids ('velvet-ants')	2
Social bees:	Hive bee	1
	Bumble bees	25
Solitary bees:	Potters	5
	Leaf-cutters	28
	Cuckoo-bees	29
	Mining and carpenter bees	101
	Others	7
Ants		36

Sub-group Parasitica	
Ichneumons (approx.)	1,800
Braconids (approx.)	900
Chalcids (approx.)	1,500
Gall-wasps or cynipids (approx.)	1,000

SUB-ORDER SYMPHYTA

Sawflies	388
Horntails	6

TABLE I.
Numbers of species of British Hymenoptera

General Characteristics of Hymenoptera

The Hymenoptera are characterised by two pairs of wings, more or less transparent and membranous, which are hooked together to act as a single pair in flight. The body is divided into head, thorax and abdomen; the head is divided from the thorax by a narrow 'neck', and bears antennae, mandibles (jaws) and suctorial mouthparts.

In the wasps there is a narrow pedicel—the 'wasp waist'—joining the thorax and the abdomen. This is actually the slender, attenuated first abdominal segment, which is more slender and attenuated in some sub-groups than in others, and which is absent in the bees, which are far more stockily built. The bees also usually have distinctively furry bodies, whereas although some species of wasps may have a few inconspicuous body hairs, most have sleek, shiny bodies. Another very important distinction is that bees gather pollen and produce beeswax and honey, which wasps do not do, with the exception of two species of wasp found in Mexico and Central America, which will be described in due course.

In the social bees, wasps and ants, besides the males and females there is also a caste of 'workers', which are sterile females; these are not found in any of the solitary species. In both social and solitary species, reproductive females ('queens') greatly outnumber the males; among the social groups the males, or 'drones', do no work in the community and are short-lived, their sole function being to fertilise the new queens.

The Hymenoptera are sub-divided into two main sub-orders, the Symphyta, which contains the sawflies and horntails, and the much larger sub-order Apocrita, which covers all the other hymenopterous insects. These include the Aculeata or true wasps, bees, ants and the so-called 'velvet-ants' which are actually wasps, and the Parasitica or gall-wasps, chalcids, braconids and ichneumons.

Among the important physiological differences between the Symphyta and the Apocrita, the former do not have the 'wasp waist' so typical of wasps, nor is the ovipositor of the female modified to form a sting. It is unfortunate that the horntails have acquired the popular name of 'wood-wasps', because they are only very distantly related to the true wasps, with which they have little in common. Apparently it is their black-and-yellow abdominal stripes which have given rise to this, but only a few of the true wasps have black-and-yellow abdominal stripes anyway, so it seems a very slender basis for this misnomer. It is rather on a par with calling crinoids—which are, of course, echinoderms and related to the starfish and sea-urchins—'sea-lilies' merely because these animals are said to have a fanciful superficial resemblance to the flowering plants of that name. Frankly, I have never yet been reminded of crinoids when seeing lilies in the garden; but the imagination of some persons stretches like elastic.

The sawflies (which, like the horntails, are outside the scope of this book) are not, of course, true flies, which have two wings only. As in the horntails, there is no 'wasp waist', and the female ovipositor is not modified to form a sting. Many of their larvae are preyed upon by various wasps for provisioning their nests with food for their grubs, which, unlike bee grubs, are carnivorous—another important difference between wasps and bees.

Definition of social behaviour

A very large proportion of the wasps—as well as of the bees—and all ants, are *social insects*, and we should now look briefly at the definition of social behaviour which differentiates between these and the solitary species.

Social organisation in the insects is found only in the Hymenoptera and in the Isoptera or termites, which are an entirely unrelated order; the social organisation in the termites is also quite different from that found in Hymenoptera, and need not be elaborated upon here.

The very primitive insects scatter their eggs at random; the next step up, practised by more advanced groups, is to deposit them on or near the future larval food supply, as in the case of beetles, butterflies and moths. In these groups the adults take no further interest in their young once the eggs have been laid.

The next progressive step is the *protection* of the eggs and young. The Hymenoptera furnish very good examples of the various ways in which this is accomplished, eggs being protected by cells built in tiers, or combs, in the case of the social species, while the solitary wasps and bees lay their eggs in underground burrows, mud pots and other well-protected situations. Among the Parasitica, the gall-wasps lay their eggs in plant tissues, the subsequently forming gall protecting them; some other Parasitica lay their eggs in galls already caused by other species. Ichneumons and certain other parasitic Hymenoptera such as braconids lay their eggs actually in the bodies of the host larvae, which will act as a living pabulum for the larval stage of the parasite.

Parental care of young

The next logical step is the parental care of the young. This is a very marked characteristic in the Hymenoptera–Aculeata. This parental care is seen at its highest level in the social wasps and bees and the ants, but even the solitary species provision their nests with insects and spiders, previously stung in order to paralyse but not kill them. In some cases the nest is provisioned with sufficient food to last the grub throughout its entire larval stage, while in others the female practises what is known as *progressive provisioning*, catching prey and taking it to the nest at intervals as and when required by her growing offspring. In this way the female maintains contact with her young, at least until they pupate.

It is generally accepted by naturalists that, while the progressive provisioning practised by the solitary wasps and bees may be defined as 'sub-social' behaviour and is well on the way to the full development of social behaviour, the highest expression of fully social behaviour in the insects is, by definition, when the female maintains contact not merely with the larvae of her first brood until they pupate, but with three or four successive broods right through their adult stages. The best examples of this are found among the social wasps, bees and ants, in which the queen, or matriarchal head of the community, is assisted by the many workers (sterile females) which have hatched from eggs laid by the queen and which take over all the duties involved in running the community, thus freeing her to devote her entire time to egg-laying, so that she is still head of the community even when her third or fourth broods are hatching, not only into workers but also producing the males and females needed in order to found new communities elsewhere and thus propagate the species.

Some solitary species build nests in close proximity, but this colonial nesting habit bears no relation to sociality in any shape or form. Each female builds her own individual nest, and works for the benefit of her own brood, or broods, only; there is no sharing of the work-load by more than one female. In fact, females will fight to defend their territory against all would-be usurpers. The sharing by more than one female is, as we have seen, found only in fully social species. There is no communal life of any kind among the solitary wasps or bees.

The reason for this colonial nesting habit, frequently found among *Ammophila* sand-wasps and other fossorial species, is purely and simply that a favourable nesting-site is available, and, if extensive in area, the wasps might just as well utilise it rather than forage further afield where perhaps another similarly favourable site might not present itself. When such a convenient 'housing estate' is discovered and adopted, this does not mean that 'Mrs. A' will, as it were, 'shop' for 'Mrs. B's' prey as well as her own, while 'Mrs. B' looks after 'Mrs. C's' babies as well as her own and 'Mrs. A's'. This joint effort may well, and in fact does, occur among Vespids and other social species. Normally colonial-nesting solitary females do not interfere with each other at all, but pursue an 'ignore-your-neighbour' policy.

The wasps comprise so many groups, each containing so many families, genera and species, that it would be quite impossible within the scope of a single book to describe all of them. I shall therefore, within this limited scope, describe some of the most interesting representatives of each group, covering as many families, genera and species as possible from all parts of the world, in an attempt to give some idea of the vast diversity of the life-histories and habits of the fascinating creatures which inhabit a world as yet largely unknown and unexplored—the world of the wasp.

CHAPTER II

The Paper Makers: The British Social Vespids

THE paper nest-building wasps or Vespidae include the hornet (*Vespa crabro*) and the familiar black-and-yellow striped *Vespula* species in Britain, as well as the vast diversity of *Polistes*, *Polybia*, *Ropalidia* and other tropical species which construct huge and elaborate nests inhabited by communities comprising thousands of individuals. These are the true social wasps, of which we shall endeavour to describe some representative groups, families, genera and species in detail. Since the British reader will be more familiar with the vespids indigenous to these islands, we shall discuss these before dealing with the more numerous and varied examples from tropical countries.

The British Vespids
The hornet (Vespa crabro)

Because it is the largest of the British Vespidae, the hornet has acquired a fearsome reputation as a ferocious attacker of humans. The propensity of the human race for attributing savage qualities to animals merely on account of their size is little founded in fact; after all, some of the deadliest creatures are small ones such as the black widow spider, which is little more than an inch long and from whose bite many people die every year. The rat is not a large animal compared with, say, a rhinoceros, but infinitely more people are killed by rats than by rhinoceroses, which at least do not carry bubonic plague. Many much smaller, even microscopic, organisms are also vectors of fatal diseases such as sleeping sickness and bilharzia.

21

The hornet is certainly considerably larger than the common *Vespula* species, but fewer people have been stung by the hornet than by its smaller relatives. It must be admitted that a contributing factor could possibly be the fact that the hornet is less commonly met with than the *Vespula* species, but this is not really important. The fact is that, by and large, the hornet is far less aggressive than *Vespula*, in direct contradiction of its popular image.

Apart from its superior size, the hornet is not really greatly different physiologically from its smaller relatives. The yellow-and-black stripes are slightly less bright, and it has a propensity for nesting in hollow trees, which the commoner *Vespula* species do not do.

In the literature there is an account of a naturalist who inadvertently snapped in half the branch of a dead tree as he was exploring a wood. The community of about twenty hornets rushed out from the interior of the broken branch in whose hollow recesses they had built their nest. When they emerged from the branch they did not, as might have been popularly supposed, buzz angrily round the naturalist, but instead buzzed busily around the broken branch, apparently inspecting the damage caused to their nest and, as it were, conferring how best to remedy the damage. The naturalist who had so rudely disturbed them was not attacked in any way. It is probable that the hornets rebuilt their nest in the upper part of the branch which was still in contact with the trunk of the tree.

The hornet is not so common as it used to be. It is difficult to account for this with any certainty, because decaying hollow trees in woods are very little affected by pollution, building or other factors which change or destroy the environment, and the food of the hornet is the same as that of *Vespula* species, merely the quantity being increased. There is certainly no diminution in the number of *Vespula* wasps around, rather the reverse.

Occasionally a hornets' nest (see Fig. 1) is built under the eaves of the roof of a house, but this is an exception rather than the rule. The normal site for a hornets' nest is in a hollow tree trunk, especially in rotting and decayed trees. If the decaying process has not reached a very advanced stage, the hornets will rasp off the wood inside so as to make a larger space in which to build the nest and, in such cases, they will construct the usual paper envelope, although the nest walls will, of course, be made of paper, like those of all other wasps of this group. When the tree trunk selected is a large one in an advanced stage of decay, the space available inside is usually too large to allow the nest to be built without the paper envelope, which is constructed from rotten wood pulp and occasionally even mixed with sand, soil or other substances to strengthen it.

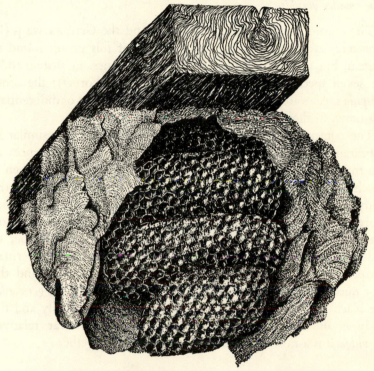

Fig. 1. The nest of the hornet *Vespa crabro* built under a beam

The nest itself may be eighteen inches in depth and a foot across, but a good many are smaller than this. The interior arrangements of combs and walls is exactly the same as in *Vespula*, but of course on a larger scale. It is also worthy of note that the hornet community does not consist of so many individuals as the communities of *Vespula* species.

Entomologists who go in for sugaring for moths at night (myself included) have noted hornets on occasions visiting the sugar patches and joining in with the moths to imbibe the sweet liquid. On no occasion—in my own experience at any rate—have hornets ever attempted to attack the hand which was busily removing moths from the sugar, or shown any other aggressive signs.

The smaller vespids

The common wasp (*Vespula vulgaris*) and the German wasp (*V. germanica*) are the two commonest wasps of this group found in Britain, but they are by no means the only ones. In Britain there are seven species of social wasp (including the hornet); the other *Vespula* species are less commonly met with and ways of differentiating between them will be described.

The common wasp and the German wasp are rather similar in appearance, but can easily be distinguished by the differences in the markings of the abdomen (see Fig. 2). As usual, the queen is much larger than the workers or the males. The black bands on the body of *V. germanica* are thicker and joined along the median line; there are usually fewer spots on the sides than in the common wasp, which generally has a larger abdomen and the number of spots on each side is four, as compared with two on the German wasp. However, the number of spots varies somewhat, and the best means of positive identification is the fact that in *V. germanica* the black abdominal bands are wider and joined centrally and the body is also more stockily-built than that of its near relative; *V. vulgaris* is a much slenderer-looking insect altogether.

The common wasp (*Vespula vulgaris*)

The nest of the common wasp is usually built underground. It is almost globular in shape, and the paper from which it is constructed is greyish in colour and fine-textured. If additions are made to the exterior, these are usually scallop-shaped, regular and beautifully textured.

About a hundred and fifty years ago Edgeworth, who made a

special study of this species, said that ninety per cent of the nests he found were built in close proximity to the nests of humble-bees, and that the two species did not interfere with each other at all. His assumption was that the wasps first adopt the nest-site, the bees coming later and building their nest near that of the wasps as a measure of protection from their chief enemy the fieldmouse which, while it would not worry unduly about a colony of bees, would be more likely to avoid stirring up the animosity of a large wasp community.

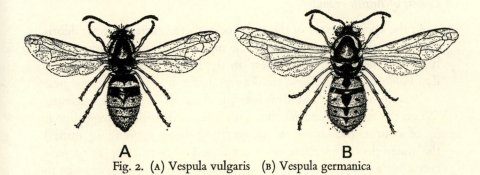

A   B

Fig. 2. (A) Vespula vulgaris   (B) Vespula germanica

There may be a good deal of truth in this assumption, because many naturalists who have collected and studied wasps in the tropics have recorded the frequency with which birds and other small arboreal creatures make their nests in large trees in close proximity to vespid wasps' nests and tree ants' nests. This is thought to provide a degree of security against marauding monkeys and tree snakes, which would hesitate to encroach upon the wasps' territory. When I was in West Africa I remember seeing a large number of social weaver birds nesting in the same tree as a very large nest of a *Polistes* species. Neither the birds nor the wasps took the slightest notice of each other as they went about their daily lives.

Getting back to the familiar British vespids, by the middle of the summer large numbers of workers have reached maturity, and as they take over from the queen the nest becomes a very busy hive—if I may use this word—of activity. The extension of the original combs and the building on of new ones takes place with increasing rapidity, in order to keep pace with the apparently unlimited egg-laying capacity of the queen. The cells which have just been vacated by emerging new workers are cleaned out and re-used with exemplary economy. By counting the number of cells in a comb and taking into consideration the fact that most of them have been used and re-used up to three times, it may be calculated that a nest containing, say, seven combs, may during one season have produced between twenty-five thousand and thirty thousand wasps.

Guests of British vespids

At the apex of some of the older cells there is usually some débris left which the workers appear to be unable to reach, but every nest has a very large staff of 'cleaners' in the form of the girdled drone-fly, *Volucella inanis*. These two-winged flies live in the wasps' nest and consume the refuse, thus leaving the cells clean and hygienic. When the female *Volucella* enters the nest to deposit her eggs (for it is, of course, the larvae which perform these scavenging duties) the wasps do not interfere with her in any way and appear to welcome her entrance into their domain. She is somewhat wasp-like in appearance, with her black-and-yellow striped body, but her shape is entirely different from that of her hosts, and she has of course only two wings instead of the wasp's four, so it is inconceivable that the wasps imagine she is one of them.

Another creature which invades the nests of both *Vespula vulgaris* and *V. germanica* is the beetle *Metocus paradoxus*. Unfortunately for the wasps, this creature, unlike *Volucella*, does absolutely nothing to help them in any way but is a predator, making its way to the cells and feeding upon the wasp grubs. The beetle is blue-black in colour and small in size, the newly-hatched larvae being only about one-fiftieth of an inch long. A strange fact emerges. The female *Metocus* lays her eggs *outside* the wasps' nest, and on hatching the larvae crawl in themselves, or gain entry by clinging to the body of a returning wasp.

The life-history of the *Metocus* larva is remarkable. It usually selects a wasp grub which is fairly well-grown, and then bores into its body just behind the head. It does not kill it, but feeds on its body fluids and fat, leaving the vital organs till last so that the hapless grub will not die but continue to supply it with sustenance. By this time the parasite has grown to about ten times its original size, when it burrows out of the skin of the wasp grub and moults. It now does a smart about-turn and attaches itself to the underside of the grub, again boring a hole into its body, and, vampire-like, sucking its life-blood. Once more it emerges, and moults again. It now proceeds to eat the remainder of its victim, finally killing it by consuming the vital organs. The *Metocus* larva then pupates, and very soon emerges as an adult beetle. Its life-history is very short, taking only one week from the egg to the pupal stage. Because of the activities of *Metocus* and certain other parasites which also live in the wasps' nest at the expense of their hosts, the wasp population is kept at a natural level by the balance of nature.

The German wasp (*Vespula germanica*)

The German wasp is equally as plentiful as its near relative above described, and I have already pointed out the differences in their appearance sufficiently to enable the field student to recognise it.

The nesting habits of the German wasp are also rather different, although it has been known to use an already existing underground burrow for its nest, such as an abandoned rabbit-hole. It prefers to use a rafter in a room, or a beam in a shed or outhouse, as a foundation for its nest; such a situation also provides a good degree of protection as well as much easier access than the narrow entrance provided by a hole in the ground. The nest of this species is usually rounder than that of the preceding species, especially in the case of nests built under roofs, and the combs are also wider. The paper of which the nest is constructed is also much more uniform in its dull grey colour, and any additions to the exterior are usually flatter and less shell-shaped than those made by *Vespula vulgaris*. These features usually serve to distinguish the nests of the two species.

Like the preceding species, the German wasp has its own special drone-fly nest scavenger, the species in this case being *Volucella pellucidens*. It is, of course, the larvae of the fly that clean the cells. This particular drone-fly is less wasp-like in appearance than

V. inanis, and is banded with narrow black-and-white stripes. Nests of *Vespula germanica* examined after being abandoned in the autumn are frequently found to be swarming with the larvae of this drone-fly, still assiduously cleaning out all the cells, even though these will not be used again. Until a few years ago it was supposed that these larvae were predatory upon the wasp grubs, until their true nature was eventually proved.

The rufous wasp (Vespula rufa)

Why this wasp was so named is hard to understand, because there is no red tinge anywhere on its body. The stripes are dull yellow which, perhaps, in very old specimens could possibly be described as dull orange; but by no stretch of the imagination could they be described as red. The hairs on the body are black; in fact this wasp has many more body hairs than either of the two preceding species, the overall effect of this being to dull its coloration.

Vespula rufa has a much earlier nesting season than either the common wasp or the German wasp and usually builds its nest underground. The general shape of the nest is much less symmetrical, and any exterior additions are usually fixed down along the edges instead of remaining open. The species is widely distributed and fairly common, but is frequently confused with the preceding two despite its smaller size and more sombre colouring.

The cuckoo wasp (Vespula austriaca)

The cuckoo wasp is very like the rufous wasp in appearance, but differs from it in a very important particular—no workers are known, only males and females. Its popular name of 'cuckoo wasp' derives from its habit of living as a lodger in the nest of the rufous wasp; it builds no nest itself, but foists it larvae upon the unsuspecting workers of that species, which, like all good adoptive mothers, bring up the cuckoo wasp larvae as their own. At least the cuckoo wasps' presence has no adverse effect upon the rufous wasp community.

The tree wasp (*Vespula sylvestris*)

The tree wasp builds her nest only in trees, and is much less common than any of the other British vespids here described. It also has a marked preference for very dry situations.

Both this species and the Norwegian wasp next to be described may be immediately distinguished from all other vespids by the antennae, which have a yellow line along the edge absent in all the other species. The markings on the body of this and the next species are very similar, but the banding is very variable in the present species. There are no spots on the abdominal segments, and the body has a very shiny appearance.

The very small nest is beautifully and symmetrically constructed and contains few cells when first built. The almost spherical envelope protecting the nest is thin and incredibly delicate-looking, tapering below to a small opening for the entrance and exit of the wasps. The nest usually bears lighter and darker rings of grey, showing how regularly the work of nest extension is carried out, making complete circles. Sometimes two or three outer walls are made, rather like the fly-sheet of a tent; this, of course, serves to protect the frail structure from inclement weather.

When the first workers emerge they assist the queen by building more and broader combs to provide her with more cells for her eggs. The new cells are built in continuous rings, and exterior additions are shell-shaped patches, as seen in the nests of other vespids.

The Norwegian wasp (*Vespula norvegica*)

This species is commoner than the preceding, and may be identified immediately by its much darker colour. This is caused by the black stripes on the abdomen being wider than in any other species, almost obscuring the yellow bands. The yellow is not bright and clear, but rather dirty-looking. There is, as in the preceding species, a yellow line along the edge of the antennae, but it is very narrow and only visible on close examination. A distinctive feature in the male is a large orange spot at each end of the black stripe on the second abdominal segment.

The nest is not unlike that of the preceding species, but the queen prefers low bushes to trees as a nest-site; it is only rarely that this wasp has been found nesting in a more elevated situation. One of these rare exceptions was recorded by Bignell (the inventor of the well-known Bignell beating-tray for collectors), who found a nest of *Vespula norvegica* in a horse-chestnut tree at a height of forty feet. Usually thorn-bushes of various kinds are chosen, which probably afford more protection from possible predators. The nest is not very large—usually little bigger than a cricket-ball. This species appears to be much more plentiful in the north and west of Britain than in the south and east.

We shall now look at the vespids of tropical Africa, South America and elsewhere, which not only far outnumber their modest British representatives but are far more diverse in their habits, and some of whose nests are among the most elaborate and beautiful structures to be found in the animal kingdom.

CHAPTER III

The Paper Makers: Polistes

As we have seen, although the Vespidae are one of the largest groups of the social wasps, they are represented in Britain by only seven species; members of this group are comparatively few in the temperate regions of the world. As we go further towards the tropics, however, we find that the vespid wasps are very well represented; the hotter the region, the more numerous they become both in species and numbers. Even in Southern Europe there is a dramatic increase in the variety and numbers of vespid wasps.

The sub-tropical and tropical vespids are all characterised by a very high degree of social organisation, and all build their nests of wood pulp which they make into paper of a degree of strength incredible for the small size of the little craftsmen who make it. I should perhaps say 'craftswomen' because it is only the females which engage in nest-building.

All the social insects, except the termites, are organised along the lines of a matriarchal society, as only the queen and the workers (sterile females) do any of the work involved in the running of the community. The sole function of the males is the fertilisation of the queens, and they take no part in any of the other work of the community.

The queen commences the building of the nest herself, and when she has prepared sufficient cells she lays her first eggs, one in each cell. As the grubs hatch and develop, her time is taken up in feeding them; but by the time her offspring have completed their development and emerged as adult workers, they take over the work of the nest completely, thus releasing her from the duties of collecting food and feeding her grubs. From this time onwards she does not leave the community, and devotes the rest of her time exclusively to egg-laying.

Division of labour

In tropical vespid societies—represented mainly by wasps of the genus *Polistes* and the closely-related *Polybia* species—the division of labour is very much marked among the workers, especially in large communities. Some are engaged in nest-enlargement; the nest rapidly increases in size, as indeed it must in order to accommodate the rapidly-growing number of combs of cells required for the reception of the vast numbers of eggs laid by the queen. Some of the equatorial African and South American *Polistes* and *Polybia* species build nests up to four or five feet in diameter; one I saw built in a forest tree in Guyana was more than six feet across. Shaped like a huge mushroom inverted from a branch close to the trunk, it was built right across the lower branches, some of which formed an integral part of the supporting structure. On further examination, I found that the nest had been abandoned fairly recently for some reason; there was not a wasp in sight, although there were the remains of dead grubs in some of the cells, in the process of being consumed by ants. Some of these very large nests may contain anything up to eleven thousand cells in the combs.

Another division of the workers carries out all the duties of cleaning the nest. The bodies of dead grubs, the remains of food and other debris are removed from the nest and deposited at a distance from it. Other individuals are employed as sentinels to keep a lookout for predators, and should a potential enemy such as a lizard or tree frog threaten the security of the nest, these wasps will band together and sting it to death.

The temperature in the interior of the nest is kept more or less constant by the activities of another group of workers which raise or lower the temperature of the interior by fanning the nest with their wings, thus reducing the temperature when it is too hot. Should the temperature drop below the requisite minimum (which is unlikely in these regions of the world) they vibrate their wings rapidly and generally keep moving in order to generate heat.

By far the greater proportion of the workers, however, are engaged in feeding the grubs which, in a well-established community, may number hundreds or even thousands, in varying stages of development. This quest for food is ceaseless and unremitting, and the workers responsible for this prime duty lead a very active life, as in some cases they have to fly considerable distances in their foraging expeditions. Unlike the solitary wasps, which provision their nests beforehand, no such provisioning is carried out by the social wasps; indeed this would be impossible, considering the vast quantity of the progeny to be catered for.

There are more than one hundred and fifty known species of *Polistes* wasps inhabiting the tropics. Owing to the favourable climatic conditions there is no dormant period of hibernation as in the case of species inhabiting temperate regions, and the very slight seasonal differences in external temperature as between wet and dry seasons leave the wasp community apparently unaffected. Without the necessity for storing up food against winter conditions, life for tropical wasps moves at a leisurely pace. The life-cycle may be repeated more than once in a year because, owing to the high temperature, the duration of the early stages is shorter. The main times of activity are in the early morning and late afternoon, as is usually found with tropical animals, the majority of which seem to require a rest period in the hottest part of the day.

In some tropical areas where there is a marked difference between the wet and dry seasons, as in monsoon areas, some *Polistes* species stop breeding during the dry season, when all their activities are somewhat reduced, although this never approaches the degree of seasonal suspension common to wasps of temperate regions. In the temperate zone, with *Polistes* species, the beginning of nest-building usually occurs at the same time each year, but there is no special season for nest-building or breeding with the equatorial *Polistes* and *Polybia* wasps, which may be found in all stages of development at any time of the year.

Field observations tend to support the view that the length of the life-cycle of the community as a whole depends mainly on the reproductive age of the queen; the first sign of a declining *Polistes* colony—which the adults are gradually abandoning—is the cessation of egg-laying by the queen. As soon as the queen is no longer the decisive factor in the community, the workers will soon lose interest, and the nest gradually falls into disuse. It is quite common to find several very small newly-formed nests near the site of the original community, even though the latter has not yet ceased functioning. Figure 3 shows an old nest of *Polistes orientalis* from India with a new nest built in close proximity on the same branch.

These new nests are built by young queens who, unlike the vespids of temperate zones in which only one queen dominates a single nest, frequently collaborate in the founding of a new colony, not only among themselves but also gathering around them a swarm of workers. Sometimes young queens from the new nests will visit the old nest nearby to see whether they can find any food which has not been taken up by the grubs.

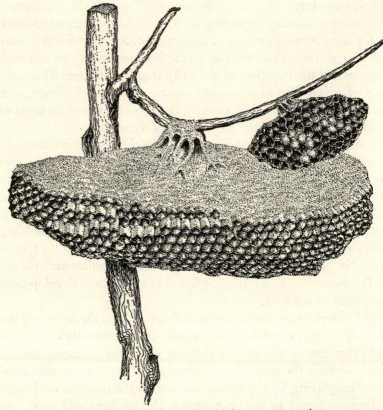

Fig. 3. Nest of *Polistes orientalis* showing new colony

Development of eggs and grubs

Unlike the bees, in which certain cells are reserved for the brood and others are used for the storage of honey and pollen, all the cells in *Polistes* nests are brood cells. The egg is attached to the cell wall nearest the nest centre, and takes about fourteen days to hatch into a grub. The grub is a legless maggot, and its entire existence is orientated to the intake of vast quantities of food. When it is fully grown, the sides of its body touch all the walls of the cell.

The workers feed the grubs by knocking their heads against the edge of the cell in order to summon the attention of the grub, which responds by extending its body as far as it will go, and bringing its mouthparts as near to the opening of the cell as possible. The adult wasp feeds the grub by literally pushing food into its face. The grub then exudes a drop of saliva on to the food, which it then takes into its jaws, releasing it from the jaws of the worker so that the latter may pass on to the next cell whose inmate requires attention. The feeding response of the grub may be artificially stimulated, as has been shown by experiments in which the wall of the entrance to the cell is tapped with the head of a pin, when the grub will appear with jaws extended.

In the course of experiments with *Polistes* wasps, the workers have been observed to imbibe drops of liquid from the mouthparts of the grubs when feeding them. The first observer to record this was the French naturalist Deleurance, who described it, in 1916, in a paper on African *Polistes* wasps which has now become a classic. He considered that this exchange of materials between workers and grubs was a vital factor in the life of the community, and later observers have put forward the theory that the substance exuded by the grubs has a high protein content, which reinforces the strength of the workers which have to lead such an active life collecting food and feeding the numerous broods. This idea has been extensively discussed in a book published in 1923 by William Morton Wheeler called *Social Life among the Insects*. The general consensus of opinion now is that the role of the larval fluid in the social life of the wasp is not yet fully understood, and so any generalisations with regard to its possible function must be treated with a certain degree of reserve.

In 1952 two other naturalists studied *Vespula sylvestris*, the European tree-wasp, and observed that these wasps also obtain drops of fluid from their grubs. The observers obtained samples of this fluid and offered them to adult wasps, along with water and other kinds of liquids such as sugar solutions in various strengths, and their findings were that the adult wasps were no more attracted to the larval fluid than they were to the other solutions offered. The observers therefore concluded that this fluid may possibly be a form of excretion, which is a plausible enough theory when one takes into consideration the fact that the grub does not possess a hindgut. However, subsequent chemical analysis revealed that these liquids do not contain any nitrogenous wastes, which rather knocks the 'excretion' theory on the head. Some further studies, as yet inconclusive, have suggested that enzymes are present in this fluid which are needed by the adults to enable them to produce certain hormones or other substances in their own bodies. Be this as it may, the habit is not universal among social wasps, and it is even less in evidence among the bees. Indeed, one large group of bees seal their larvae up in their cells with a food supply, and there is therefore no contact between the grubs and the adults.

Food foraging in Polistes

A typical day in the life of a newly-emerged *Polistes* worker consists of about twenty trips foraging for food. The first few trips will be undertaken for the purpose of familiarising herself with the location of her nest. These wasps have been observed to stand and stare, as it were, for prolonged periods at conspicuous landmarks near the nest site in order to imprint them on their memory and thus enable them to find the nest without difficulty on returning from a food-gathering foray.

Experiments have been carried out by various observers to assess the ability or otherwise of newly-emerged *Polistes* wasps to find the nest after they have first been removed and released some distance away from it. If they have not first been allowed to make this reconnaissance flight, they very seldom find their way back. In other experiments, nests have been removed from their original site and planted elsewhere to see how the wasps will behave. If they were allowed to make this reconnaissance flight first, they almost invariably found it again easily, but if they were not so allowed, they rarely returned.

The *Polistes* worker forages for four different purposes: to find wood fibre to make paper pulp for nest-building; to find insects to feed the grubs; to find nectar either for her own use or to feed the grubs; and to bring water to the nest. Wasps, unlike the bees, never collect pollen, although, of course, they may unwittingly transfer it from one flower to another while searching for insects. Hunting wasps are usually so preoccupied with what they are looking for that they rarely sting, even if they are disturbed.

When *Polistes* wasps spot caterpillars or other insects suitable as food for their grubs, they appear to become very excited, buzzing around the branches or plants, and then making a bee-line—if I may use this term—for the prey. They grasp this in their jaws and, if it is small enough, fly off with it at a fast speed. If it is too big to be so transported, they usually sting it to death and then remove parts of it to be transported to the nest, returning for the remainder later. By masticating the food with their jaws they can reduce its bulk, enabling them to transport more of it at a time than they could otherwise do.

Polistes workers are always willing to wait for one another, and have even been observed to relieve one another of their burdens. On returning to the nest with a large insect for food, the worker is frequently met at the nest entrance by one or more of her nest-mates, who will commence to chew at the load until it is able to be separated into two or more portions which they can easily carry in to the grubs. On occasions two or three workers have been seen to eat the food themselves instead of feeding it to the grubs, and have had to fly off again to bring more!

When wood fibre is brought in for paper-making, the loads are frequently so large and unwieldly that one worker often transfers her load to two or more others in its entirety. The probable reason for this is because an unbroken pulp-load would be stronger for nest-building purposes than several small pieces would be.

The amount of nectar fed to the grubs varies not so much according to species but more according to the availability of the source of supply. In tropical South America certain wasps of this group are pests of the sugar-cane boiling factories, and will fly off with portions of the crude sugar if they can get to it. Before the invention of insecticides, the vertical combs of *Polistes* wasps used to hang in fringes over the vats where the sugar-cane was boiled, until it became such a nuisance that people were employed specially to destroy them.

The sugar is taken to the grubs in liquid form, and deposits of this sugar where some have hardened on the cell walls are moistened by the grub with the fluid from its mouthparts earlier referred to, in order to assimilate it. Workers have also been seen putting their heads inside the cells in order to lick this sugar deposit from the cell walls.

Water requirements of Polistes

Water is required in paper-making, and where *Polistes* wasps are observed in arid regions, this is a sure sign that there is a continuous source of water somewhere nearby; if there is no stream, there may be perhaps a tank of some kind. Without water, the wasps are unable to make paper from wood. They also drink water, and have been observed drinking at puddles and other sources of standing water. On very hot days, many workers devote their time exclusively to the collection of water-drops, which are carried in the jaws, and sometimes these are deposited on both exterior and interior of the nest in an effort to reduce the temperature by evaporation, in addition to the fanning activities of other workers already referred to.

The moistening of the nest surface and the fanning of the interior make a very effective cooling system, which has been proved to serve very adequately in lowering the temperature in order to avoid overheating of the brood and decomposition of food stocks. Although normally only the workers perform services of this nature, even males and queens have occasionally been seen to contribute to this system, so great is the necessity for it to be maintained at an equable level; it would seem that they literally have no choice when workers are in short supply, such as in the case of a newly-formed nest, or in an older-established nest when almost all the workers were out hunting.

Polistes in temperate zones

The presence or otherwise of wasps and the degree of their activity is a good guide to the progress of the summer. (This, of course, does not apply to the tropics.) At the end of the breeding season the old nests are rarely re-used, and new nests will be founded by the young queens which, together with the males, emerge towards the end of the summer and in the early autumn. After fertilisation, the new queens go into hibernation, and those which survive the winter awaken with the first sunshine of spring to start the life-cycle all over again.

The first eggs laid by the new queens invariably produce workers which, as we have already seen, are sterile females. The eggs which will produce the next season's new queens, and those producing males, are laid later in the year. Therefore the bulk of the wasps which buzz in apparent anger around summer picnickers are all workers; it is very unlikely that queens will be encountered at this time, as they are normally too busy laying eggs in the nest. The males which emerge in the autumn have no sting.

When egg-laying ceases, the community begins to show signs of decline. Cells from which the brood has already emerged are not used again, and so as the season progresses increasing numbers of brood-cells will be found empty in the nest. Not only does egg-laying cease as autumn approaches; the foraging workers will find less and less food available, and many of the grubs will be allowed to starve to death. Grubs are also sometimes ejected forcibly from the nest by workers who can no longer provide for them. A few observers have sometimes recorded seeing these grubs used as food to feed other grubs, though this is not a very common practice among *Polistes* or other social wasps.

The scarcity of food as autumn approaches is reflected in the behaviour of the wasps. As the workers return to the nest with food, they are greeted at the door, as it were, with a great show of enthusiasm, seven or eight of the workers all grabbing at the same time at the food. Some workers returning empty-handed have also been seen to be mobbed by their nest-mates.

39

Mating of Polistes wasps

The mating of the males and the new queens usually takes place after the nest has been abandoned for the season. (I refer now to the *Polistes* species which inhabit the temperate regions; in tropical areas there is no special mating season.) On sunny autumn days a number of males will congregate together and set out to search for the young queens; this swarm of wasps may look quite aggressive, but since they have no sting they are perfectly harmless. They usually fly about in circles until they eventually contact the females of their choice, when they descend to ground level.

The actual mating period is so short that it has been very infrequently observed; the pair disjoin and fly off almost immediately, making it extremely difficult to photograph them, or to observe them at all. It has, however, been established that the female sting is extruded at this time; this is thought to be not a display of aggression but merely a movement to facilitate the access of the male and at the same to avoid stinging him.

After mating the new queens prepare to go into hibernation, while the males, after a few desultory flights here and there, gradually lose their strength and die. Very few males have been known to attempt to hibernate, or to survive the winter. The females in hibernation are so torpid that they appear almost dead; they are completely unresponsive to external stimuli. They can endure a temperature well below zero with no ill effects. The physiological adaptations enabling them to withstand these conditions are not completely known. They are dehydrated to a considerable extent, which probably reduces possible damage to the tissues from freezing. It has also been found that glycerine is present in small quantities in the blood, forming a natural inbuilt 'anti-freeze'.

Despite the social organisation of the paper-building wasps, the reason for their frequently hibernating in clusters is not apparent. They are certainly not huddling together to keep warm, since wasps, like all insects, are poikilothermic, which means that their body temperature is the same as that of their surroundings. In fact it would be disadvantageous for them to increase their body temperature, because they would then become active instead of conserving all the energy required for nest-building and egg-laying in the following spring. When this time comes, the groups break up, and each young queen goes off independently to found a new nest; females never join forces to do this.

CHAPTER IV

The Paper Makers: Polybia

THE tropical wasps of the genus *Polybia* form the largest group of the social species. Most are found in Central and northern South America; only a very few species penetrate into the southern United States.

The social organisation of most *Polybia* wasps varies in certain very important details from *Polistes* and other tropical vespids. The majority of them found new colonies by swarming, instead of by the more typical method adopted by most other vespids—especially those of the temperate zones—in which the fertilised young queen sets off alone to find a new nest-site and commences its construction herself, subsequently laying eggs which in due course hatch into the workers which eventually take over the duties of the nest and free the queen for egg-laying.

In *Polybia* each young fertilised queen gathers around her a large group of workers from the old nest. This constitutes the 'swarm', and they start the new nest together. Since males are never found in these new nests, it is thought that they die soon after fertilising the young queens.

Another very important difference in the social organisation of *Polybia* wasps is that in the majority of communities more than one egg-laying queen may 'reign'. There may be as few as four, or as many as one hundred, though around ten or twelve is the most usual number found in the smaller communities, with proportionately more in the larger ones.

In *Polybia* species the queens and the workers are scarcely distinguishable at sight, since there is hardly any difference in size. In certain species the queens are marginally larger overall, and the base of the abdomen is slightly broader; the abdomen of older queens may become slightly swollen after egg-laying has ceased. In the majority of species, however, the only certain way to find out whether an adult is a queen or a worker is by microscopic examination of the ovaries of a dissected specimen.

Another important difference between *Polybia* and other tropical vespids is that there appear to be two distinct types of colony. One type is what could be called a long-term project, persisting certainly for four or five years, and often—according to some unconfirmed records—considerably longer. The other type of colony is short-lived, dispersing after a few months, the inmates breaking up into new swarms. No one seems to be sure why these two distinct types of colony should occur, but nature must certainly have some very good reason for it, most probably related to different and more efficient ways of attaining maximum species dispersal.

Most *Polybia* wasps build their incredibly beautiful nests in forest trees, suspended from the branches. The outer envelope is frequently covered with lichen and moss brought to the site by the wasps and woven ingeniously into the exterior texture in such a way that they will continue to grow naturally; this camouflage renders the nest very inconspicuous, and in a well-foliated tree it is practically invisible. Considering the numbers of enemies against which *Polybia* wasps have to wage unremitting warfare, any and every way of foiling the opposition must be pressed into service. Monkeys, birds, tree snakes, tree frogs, lizards and ants are the chief predators, and they are only too ready to risk a few stings in order to obtain some juicy wasp grubs.

The ants must contribute the greatest hazard. Driver ants are immensely powerful, and a horde of them can easily destroy a large *Polybia* nest overnight. Accordingly, many *Polybia* species have given up the unequal struggle and decreed a policy of 'if you can't beat 'em, join 'em'—and have perfected what must be one of nature's most impossible achievements—to live in harmony with a colony of driver ants. These *Polybia* communities—which are of the 'long-lived colony' type—share a tree with a huge nest, or nests, of driver ants. Neither side molests the other, and this uneasy truce is shared also by birds and other small vertebrates which live in the trees, which thus enjoy the double immunity of protection from their own

43

enemies by proximity to hordes of biting ants and stinging wasps—they never had it so good! How these curious partnerships first became established is still one of nature's most closely-guarded mysteries; no one has yet come up with any theory worthy of serious consideration.

A mango tree examined by Professor O. W. Richards and his wife on their 1937 expedition to Guyana (then British Guiana) was found to house eight nests of *Polybia rejecta,* innumerable large suspended earth-and-fibre nests of the tree ant *Dolichoderus,* and several orioles' nests. Neither the birds, the ants, nor the wasps interfered with each other in any way.

In strange contrast to this comradeship-at-arms, the 'short-lived colonies' of *Polybia* have tackled the same problem in an entirely different way. A small wasps' nest can easily be overrun and destroyed by driver ants, but again, such a small nest does not represent the same amount of effort in its construction as does a large nest housing a community consisting of thousands of individuals. So if a small nest is made the target of attack by ants, the wasps will desert it at speed without so much as a backward glance, and rebuild elsewhere. In these small short-lived colonies the queens are young and their energies have not been exhausted by egg-laying, so they still have the agility to enable them to make a quick getaway; they are not nest-bound egg-producing robots, like the old queens of those vespids who have delegated all the other duties of the nest to the workers. A young and energetic queen, together with her band of loyal workers, can construct a new nest in twenty-four hours.

This has actually been seen taking place, the new nest being sited about thirty feet away from the old one which, after a raid by driver ants, was left little more than an empty shell. Professor Richards, who recorded the occurrence (in Guyana), stated that the swarm consisted of twenty-two queens and one hundred and eighteen workers, and that by the end of forty-eight hours the new nest already contained seven combs with a total of one hundred and sixty seven cells, every one of which contained an egg. Unfortunately the industry of these little *Polybias* was ill-rewarded, for hardly had the life of their new colony begun than driver ants again raided it.

The size of *Polybia* colonies varies enormously. Some never form big colonies, only a small nest being built containing a few dozen cells; sometimes only one queen and five or six workers form the little community, though on occasions two queens may collaborate. Since none of the cells in nests examined had ever contained a cocoon, it follows that the two queens had been joint foundresses of the colony and not mother and daughter.

These tiny colonies, however, are the exception rather than the rule, at least in Guyana. The findings of Professor Richards and his wife in 1937 were borne out by my own observations when I was there in 1971. Professor and Mrs. Richards found that the average *Polybia* community contained anything from fifty to one thousand wasps; my wasp-counts from average *Polybia* colonies varied from seventy-eight to nearly fifteen hundred. One nest of *Polybia rejecta* examined by the Richards team was found to contain 7,758 cells; this was populated by fourteen hundred wasps. Another larger nest contained 21,600 cells and was inhabited by 7,087 wasps, of which 93 were egg-laying queens.

When the Richards team ventured into Brazil they found many much larger *Polybia* nests, with populations in excess of ten thousand wasps. Not having visited Brazil, I cannot confirm this from personal observation, but in northern Guyana close to the Venezuelan border I did not find any appreciable difference in the average size of *Polybia* communities from those I saw in other parts of the country.

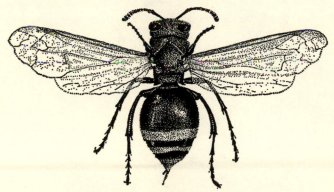

Fig. 4. Brachygastra lecheguana (×4)

Most species of *Polybia* prey upon other insects, including winged ants and termites, many of which are caught on the wing during their nuptial flight. Since these nuptial flights usually take place at definite times, the wasps usually make the most of the opportunity and catch numbers of them at one time, and store them in the nest. Some *Polybia* species forage widely throughout the forest for insects

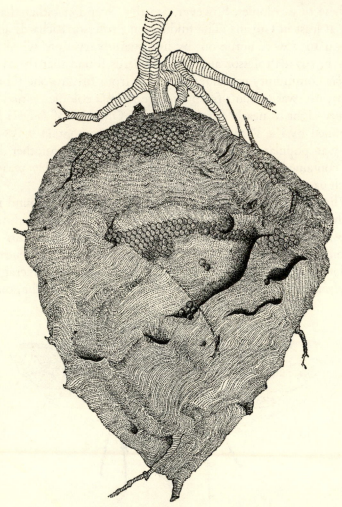

Fig. 5. Nest of *Brachygastra lecheguana*

46

of all kinds; these, Professor Richards points out, defend their nests with great ferocity and do not hesitate to sting the collector who wishes to study them not wisely but too well. I was fortunate that I was never stung, or perhaps I was just careful!

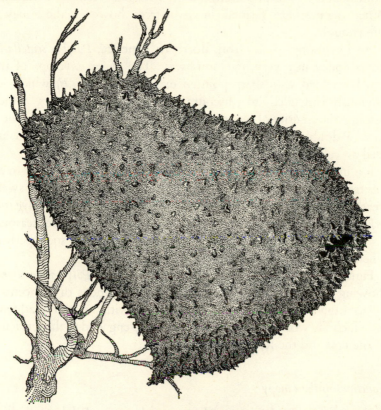

Fig. 6. Nest of *Polybia scutellaris*

Some *Polybia* wasps visit flowers and fruits and collect nectar and fruit juices. A very few are regular nectar-gatherers like the honey-bee. One closely-allied species, *Brachygastra lecheguana* (Fig. 4), has been more or less semi-domesticated in Mexico. The nests are hung in citrus-trees and allowed to grow to a certain size before the wasps are smoked out and the honey removed. If the primary foundation-pillar of the nest is left hanging from the tree, the wasps will return and rebuild the nest in the same spot. A nest of this species is shown at Figure 5.

One must exercise caution when sampling the honey of wild strains of *Brachygastra lecheguana*, as it sometimes gathers nectar from the flowers of poisonous plants, with fatal results for humans. When the nests are 'farmed' in citrus-trees, however, the honey is safe enough.

An interesting species from northern America, *Polybia scutellaris*, stores honey in a very ingenious way. The paper envelope of the nest is studded with sharp-pointed excrescences (Fig. 6) which are obviously intended to discourage would-be predators which threaten the security of the community. However, these excrescences serve a double purpose. They are hollow on the inside, and are used as 'cells' for the storage of honey.

It is interesting to note that honey-storing *Polybias* do not go to all this trouble just for the fun of it, or to provide humans with a sweet treat: nature always has a better reason than that! Both *Brachygastra lecheguana* and *Polybia scutellaris* occur in areas where seasonal droughts occur, and the honey is stored up against such periods when food is scarce in the forest.

Figure 7 shows the interior of the same nest of *Polybia scutellaris*, showing in cross-section the elaborate arrangement of the central pillars supporting the combs, interspersed with interior platforms on which the workers alight and walk while engaged in the servicing of the nest and the feeding of the brood.

Functions of the canopy

One of the most important differences between *Polybia* and allied genera and *Polistes* is that wasps of the former group build an envelope or canopy around the combs. In this particular they are like *Vespa* and *Vespula*, but although the function of the canopy is similar—i.e., not only protection but temperature-regulation—in the case of *Polybia* this insulation is required to keep the interior of the nest cooler than that of the surrounding air, as opposed to the vespids of temperate zones, in which the temperature of the nest is several degrees higher than it is outside.

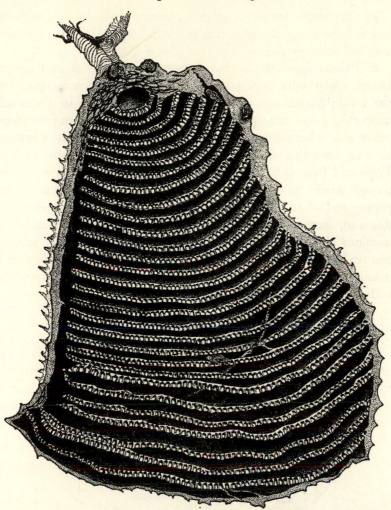

Fig. 7. Cross-section through nest of *Polybia scutellaris*, showing arrangement of combs

The canopy of the nest of many *Polybia* and allied species is multi-layered (see the cross-section of the nest of *Polybia scutellaris* at Figure 7) and this form of construction, of course, increases the insulation potential of the envelope by trapping air-pockets between the layers.

49

The envelope also serves other important functions. It shields the brood from direct sunlight, rain and wind, as well as the inevitable ants and other predators.

In *Polybia scutellaris*, at the southernmost limits of its range in Brazil, where what appear to be perennial colonies are exposed to the mild 'winter' conditions at the extreme edge of the south temperate zone, the spaces between the layers of the envelope are used as hibernacula by the overwintering wasps. It is of interest to note here that the vespids of the temperate regions, such as *Vespa* and *Vespula*, do not use the nest in which to hibernate, even though some envelopes may be constructed on a multi-layered pattern and afford convenient air-pockets. It is difficult to know why this is so, since each queen is thus compelled to find another hibernaculum elsewhere despite the existence of an apparently suitable one ready at hand. This may be, however, because the old nest is usually abandoned before the onset of cold weather, and a new nest built the following spring.

Nest architecture in Polybia and related species

The internal structure of canopied nests is almost as varied as the number of species which construct them. In a few, such as *Metapolybia*, *Synoeca* and others, the cells are built directly on the substratum to which the nest is attached, while in other species the envelope becomes, as it were, the 'backing' for cells built directly on to it,

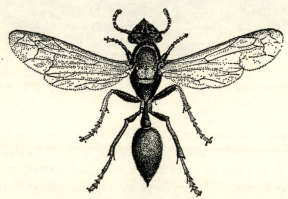

Fig. 8. Queen of *Polybia scutellaris* (×4)

or it may serve as the attachment surface for combs with pedicels.

In the longer-established colonies of some species such as *Polybioides raphigastra* and *Protopolybia pumila*, the combs may take the form of a broad spiral; in others such as *Stelopolybia angulata* they are more in the form of vertical cylinders. A spherical shape would best describe the comb construction of *Stelopolybia flavipennis*, while *Stelopolybia vicina* shares with the *Vespa* and *Vespula* wasps the familiar pattern of horizontal tiers. Parallel vertical panels are found in various species of *Polybioides*, while a variety of more complicated and less easily described forms is adopted by numerous other members of this group.

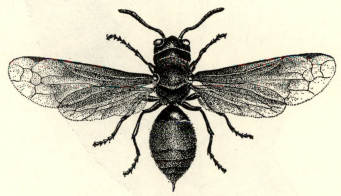

Fig. 9. *Parachartergus apicalis* (×3)

One of the most commonly-found architectural styles is that found in most species of the typical genus *Polybia*, and to a certain extent, though somewhat modified, in *Brachygastra*, *Chartergus* and one or two other genera. The nest of the well-established colony has several combs attached horizontally, without pedicels, to the canopy by the edge, and arranged in tiers, as typified by the example of *Polybia scutellaris* already referred to, whose nest in cross-section is shown at Figure 7. Figure 8 shows a queen of this species.

The wasps commence building the nest by first constructing a domed roof, usually tangential to the branch of a tree. A discoid platform is then attached below this, and the first cells are built, using this platform as a base. The roof is then extended to form the sides and bottom of the canopy, and the nest is enlarged by building

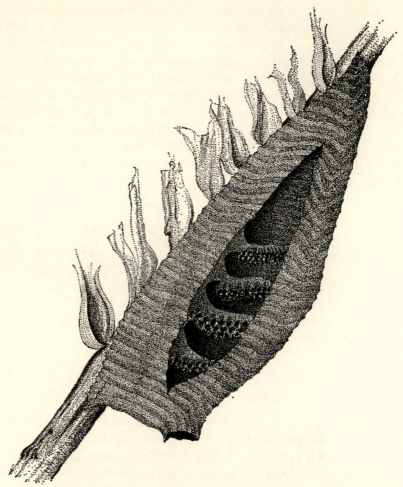

Fig. 10. Nest of *Parachartergus apicalis*, cut open to show arrangement of combs

cells on the underside of the floor, which thus forms a new roof, when the sides are again extended and the bottom closed, except for the entrance hole. Access to the comb is gained via an opening left in the centre of each, in line with the main entrance at the bottom of the nest.

The nest of *Parachartergus apicalis* (Fig. 9) from Central America is a good example of the slightly modified version of the typical

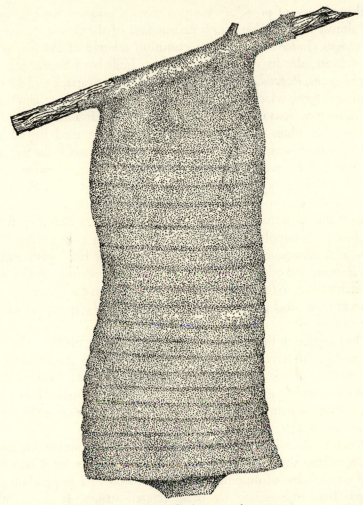

Fig. 11. Nest of *Chartergus chartarius*

Polybia arrangement. In the nest, shown at Figure 10, the outer canopy has been cut open to show the arrangement of the combs, which in this species are set at right angles to the nest support.

Nest construction and materials

The materials from which nests are constructed vary greatly

53

in their degree of proof against predators. Compare, for example, the almost impregnable tough carton nest of the South American *Chartergus chartarius* (Fig. 11), a common relative of *Polybia*, with the delicate, slender columnar structures built by a South African vespid genus, *Ropalidia* (Fig. 12), which are open to attack and devoid of any canopy—which latter feature at once distinguishes them from the enveloped nests of the *Polybia* species and their allies.

Vegetable fibres in one form or another are used by all the paper-making wasps. A few reinforce this material during the pulping process with mud, but these are in the minority. One species, *Polybia emaciata*, has been frequently quoted in the literature as being the exception to the general rule: her delicate wafer-thin canopy and beautifully-sculptured cells are fashioned entirely from mud—a most unpolybioid characteristic, if I may coin a term. The sub-social *Stenogaster* mud-nesters, which make mud nests rather like *Eumenes* and other potters, are also related to *Polybia*. A few add vegetable fibres to the mud during construction, as though unwilling to sever their most palpably apparent link with the group to which they belong.

The function of the pedicel seems to be a support for the cells, but it is thought to have evolved along lines suggesting that its original function was to ward off predators such as ants. *Polistes* workers have been seen standing guard at the proximal end of the pedicel knocking off ants, one at a time, which had the temerity to use the pedicel as a bridge to the nest.

When I was collecting in West Africa I had constant trouble from ants attacking the lepidoptera on my setting-boards, until one day I hit on the plan of dipping string in creosote and suspending the boards from the ceiling by these treated strings. It successfully foiled the ants, as well as producing such side-effects as the smell being highly off-putting to humans! I need not have been so smug, however, at outwitting the ants. Millions of years before, a tiny wasp was doing precisely the same thing.

An observer in Brazil who studied *Mischocyttarus drewseni*, which builds an uncanopied comb supported by a very long, thin pedicel, discovered that the wasps repeatedly rub the undersides of their abdomens against it. He found that these wasps have a gland on the ventral surface of the final abdominal segment which secretes a noxious substance. This, when transferred to the nest pedicel, renders it repellent to ants.

Most paper-making wasps have a so-called 'construction gland' in the head, which produces a transparent fluid used as 'size' in the

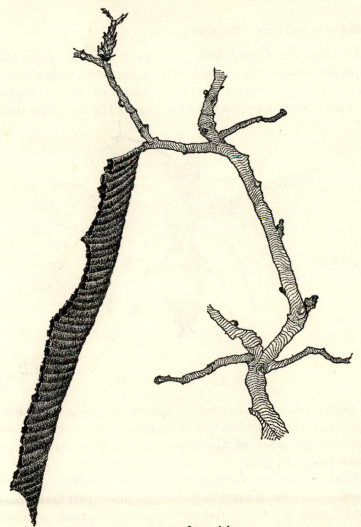

Fig. 12. Nest of *Ropalidia* sp.

preparation of nest carton from plant fibres and water. This fluid dries and hardens to form a shining, lacquer-like waterproof coating, and also helps to anchor and strengthen the pedicel of the nest. In *Metapolybia pediculata* it forms transparent mica-like 'windows' in the canopy, whose generally mottled appearance increases its camouflage potential.

Predators of Polybia and her allies

All wasps are plagued with predators of all kinds, from microscopic parasites to other wasps, bees, ants, tree frogs, snakes, birds and mammals. One observer discovered that bats are an important predator of certain *Polybia* species in Brazil. The bats chew through

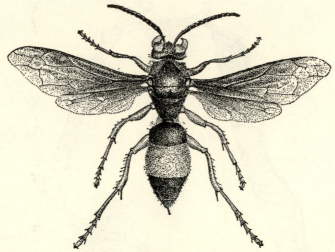

Fig. 13. *Vespa tropica* (×1¼)

the paper envelope and systematically eat the grubs, returning the following night to see whether there are any survivors. The tough cardboard-like nests of *Chartergus* species, however, are proof against attacks by bats.

Guard females are frequently posted at the nest entrances of various species, and if a rent should appear in any part of the canopy, guard females will station themselves there at the ready to ward off predators while the workers are repairing it.

Other wasps, particularly the larger species, frequently prey upon their smaller relatives. *Vespa tropica* (Fig. 13), a huge species with a three-inch wing-span, is reported to prey exclusively upon the grubs and pupae of various *Polistes* and *Polybia* species, at least in some parts of its range.

Nest defence is an important part of community life. In some species of both *Polybia* and *Polistes* the entire outer nest surface is covered at night by dense clusters of sleeping wasps, their stinging ends pointing aggressively in the direction of any outsider who may threaten the security of the helpless brood within. A nocturnal wasp, *Apoica*, builds uncanopied nests, and in the daytime these wasps sleep on the external nest surface, covering the vulnerable comb with their bodies. It would be virtually impossible for even a small intruder to reach the brood without touching and alerting an adult—and since the entire nest is literally bristling with stings, it is unlikely to try!

A *Synoeca* species from Surinam, which is a metallic blue-black, is well-protected. When disturbed these wasps produce a rhythmic drumming sound by vibrating their thin nest-envelope from within; this warning noise is audible at a distance of several yards. If the disturbance is increased, the entire colony rushes out in a body, and continues the drumming on the outside of the nest, raising and lowering their wings and threatening the intruder with their stings. Since *Synoeca* is one of the very few wasps to possess a barbed sting like that of a bee, which is left in the wound after attack, these wasps are doubly protected.

Some wasps, however, have gone to the other extreme and, as we have seen, rely on the protection afforded by building their nests in trees inhabited by *Dolichoderus* and other fierce and aggressive ants. These wasps include *Polybia rejecta*, *P. lugubris*, *Stelopolybia pallipes*, and some *Mischocyttarus* species. One of the latter, however, in contrast, exhibits non-aggressive defence behaviour. This wasp is *Mischocyttarus fitzgeraldi*, which falls to the ground shamming dead when disturbed, 'recovering' and flying off when the hostile stimulus has disappeared.

It seems that, in a world where 'eat or be eaten, kill or be killed' is the inexorable law of survival, the wasps have a harder life than the bees, who quietly forage for pollen and honey without the necessity of putting up a fight to get it. The predators of bees—which, incidentally, include certain wasps—are more insidious, most of them being parasitic and laying their eggs in an unattended nest, rather than engaging in combat with their prey, which wasps are more likely to do. The social structure of the paper-making wasps, however, affords a great degree of 'safety in numbers'—sometimes very considerable numbers.

In a very different position, however, are the solitary wasps, which must rely on their own resources to outwit their enemies. We shall now take a look at some of them, to see how ingeniously many of them have managed to adapt themselves to overcome the limitations of a non-socially-orientated existence.

CHAPTER V

The Solitary Wasps: Ammophila

THE word *Ammophila* means literally 'sand-loving', and the group of solitary wasps bearing this generic name comprises a very large number of species. Most *Ammophila* wasps are of comparatively large size, and these wasps have the narrowest 'wasp waist' of all solitary wasps. They have to, to render the abdomen mobile enough to perform all kinds of acrobatic contortions in order to sting their caterpillar victims in the elaborate manner typical of the genus. All *Ammophila* wasps are caterpillar-predators, and, as such, they need to adopt rather different techniques from those employed by their cricket- and grasshopper-hunting relations to be later described.

Nest-building in Ammophila

The majority of the solitary wasps are ground-nesters and the Ammophilids dig their burrows in sandy places. Fabre noticed that when certain *Ammophila* species were digging their burrows they would remove unwanted stones for some little distance, and put them aside. The sand is excavated with the forelegs, which are provided with combs and bristles. These are used synchronously, not alternately as in the Pompilids (see Chapter XII). Before going off hunting, *Ammophila* closes her burrow temporarily, frequently with a flat stone of appropriate size, and these are the ones which have been seen to be put aside while digging.

The observer Baerends saw an *Ammophila* wasp trying out various stones for size, as it were, placing them in position one after another and rejecting them, before finally deciding on one which was just right. Sand and pine needles are frequently brought and used to complete the temporary blockage of the mouth of the burrow, and it has been suggested that the use of these materials, placed in a particular way, may also help the wasp to identify the entrance to her own individual nest when returning from a hunting foray. Final closure is quite elaborate in *Ammophila*, and many observers have recorded that in order to achieve a firm closure some species not only pound the stones with their heads but also grasp a pebble in their jaws and use it as a battering-ram to consolidate the blockage. *Ammophila* wasps have also been seen rearranging the stones at the entrance to the shaft to their liking. While some species appear to use these techniques regularly, others apparently never do.

Orientation is very important to Ammophilid wasps; usually when the digging has been completed the female will fly around for a little while, as though to commit the details of the immediate neighbourhood of the nest to memory. Occasionally digging will be interrupted while such a reconnaissance is carried out. Some wasps seem to learn after one short lookout flight, while others take longer and require more flights before a memory-pattern is established. The learning of landmarks is usually carried out during flight, and not while the wasp is engaged in dragging the prey along the ground to her burrow.

Occasionally some wasps seem to be much less able to find their way home than others; one *Ammophila pubescens* was observed dragging her caterpillar victim with her the entire time she spent looking in vain for her burrow, which she eventually found again after an hour. Ford carried out experiments in which he placed metal screens in the path of an *Ammophila pubescens* returning with prey to her nest. The wasp invariably and unhesitatingly diverged just sufficiently to get round the obstacle, and then resumed her proper course. This species is a particularly good navigator; it has to be, because it usually keeps two or three nests on the go at once, using the method of progressive provisioning.

A curious fact has emerged while observers have watched Ammophilid wasps at their various activities. Many species do not normally use their burrows to sleep in; these are closed from the outside, so that the wasps have to 'sleep out', as it were. They may be found fast asleep clinging to grass-stems by their jaws—which would seem an extremely uncomfortable alternative to sleeping in a cosy burrow protected from the weather and from predators.

Sandy commons and gravel-pits are among the best places to look for Ammophilid wasps. Some of the pioneer English hymenopterists at the end of the last century did a great deal of their collecting on the sandy commons surrounding London, mainly in Surrey, and a good many of the rarer species they discovered at that time can still be found there, but some of them have disappeared from their former haunts. Sand-dunes by the coast also provide a habitat for certain species, but the difference in habitat between an inland sandy bank and a coastal strip of sand-dunes supports different habitat-specific species with very little overlapping, even within the same genera. A very few members of this group have quite different habits, building their nests in holes in wood, or in the stems of brambles and other plants, so it is difficult to visualise these particular species as members of the same group as the essentially and predominantly sand-burrowing Ammophilids.

Food preferences in Ammophila and related species

The Ammophilids' tastes in caterpillars differ according to species. The indefatigable Fabre was the first to observe that one particular species caught only the larvae of Geometrid moths, known as 'loopers' because of their way of looping their bodies while walking.

Podalonia, which is closely related to *Ammophila*, specialises only in caterpillars of *Noctua segetum*, the turnip moth. The larvae of this moth live underground and feed on turnips and other rootcrops. How the wasp detects the presence of the larva is unknown, though, presumably, it makes use of its antennae as a kind of 'geiger counter'. Be this as it may, the wasp proceeds to burrow down and dig the turnip moth grub out of the root in which it is feeding; the wasp then stings the grub, and bears it in triumph to her burrow.

Ammophila campestris has been observed to take sawfly larvae, apparently in mistake for those of lepidoptera. The larvae of sawflies are superficially not unlike moth larvae and although it is easy for a lepidopterist to tell them apart by the differences in the number of prolegs, it would seem that *Ammophila campestris* is unable to do so and occasionally slips up. Probably sawfly and moth larvae taste different, so that *Ammophila* is wiser after the event! All *Ammophilids* carry their caterpillar victims belly upwards, usually dragging them along the ground by the legs, but one or two have been seen carrying them in low flight.

The Peckhams in America watched *Ammophila urnaria* drag a caterpillar along the ground for 260 feet, taking more than two hours. *Ammophila pubescens* was seen 'flying while carrying small larvae, but dragging larger ones along the ground': this does not really surprise me!

Wheeler and Evans have remarked that the genus *Ammophila* is of particular interest to the student of evolution, as it includes examples of different kinds of behaviour within a single genus. Thus, some use a single larva to provision the nest, while others provision their nests with several larvae. Again, we have Ammophilids in which provisioning is delayed: the mass of their prey is brought after the egg hatches. Then, again, there are others which regularly employ progressive provisioning, and finally, as we have already seen in the case of *Ammophila pubescens*, there are a few species which even keep several nests going simultaneously.

Baerends has made particularly interesting observations on this latter species, which, by the way, is the only solitary wasp in which progressive provisioning has been observed. Baerends noted an *Ammophila pubescens* working at three holes in turn, in each of which provisioning was at different stages, having been commenced on different days. The female visited each nest at the beginning of the day's operations, and evidently determined how many caterpillars would be required to satisfy the needs of the grubs in their various stages of development. Apparently, according to Baerends's observations, when the wasp had discovered how many caterpillars were required for one particular burrow she would spend the remainder of that day in stocking up that burrow. Baerends would sometimes before this daily visit add to the store of larvae, or remove some; the wasp would then modify her actions accordingly, and food would be brought where it was most needed. If, however, Baerends added or removed caterpillars *after* the wasp had completed her morning round of inspection, this subsequent interference would be completely ignored, and food would be brought according to what the morning inspection had revealed as necessary, entirely disregarding the quantity of caterpillars present in the burrow after the wasp had left.

The varying habits of *Ammophila* wasps are so fascinating that it seems quite strange to discover that they have not been the subject of so many experiments as other Sphecids. One, however, comes to mind. Another observer has recorded that she waited until an *Ammophila* had completed her provisioning and effected a final closure to the nest. The observer then offered the wasp another paralysed caterpillar. The wasp promptly reopened the nest but, finding it satisfactorily provisioned, reclosed it. The observer offered another caterpillar, with the same result; but a third offer was rejected, and the wasp flew off.

Fabre experimented by trying to switch the diet of *Ammophila* and related species. Most *Ammophila* wasps offered insects other than caterpillars refused them, and took an interest only in caterpillars, but Fabre was able to rear *Ammophila holosericea* on a diet of small spiders in captivity, and he also managed to persuade a *Podalonia hirsuta* grub to take an adult black cricket. These deviations from the norm would, however, appear to be few and far between. One is bound to arrive at the conclusion that the extreme specificity of the diet of many of these wasps is determined rather at the level of the hunting habits of the adults than concerned with larval preferences.

Recognising some British Ammophilids

The student of British Ammophilid wasps will find no difficulty in recognising our largest and handsomest sand wasp, *Ammophila sabulosa* (Fig. 14). A really large female can be an inch in body length. The head, thorax and part of the first abdominal segment are black; the remainder of the abdomen, except the tip which is black, is a sandy-ochreous hue (not 'red' as maintained by some authorities).

The male may be distinguished from the female by a small black spot on both first and second abdominal segments; these spots are absent in the female. The female, too, has a distinctive feature not found in her mate: a number of hairs on the sides of the final abdominal segment, which are easily visible without a hand-lens.

This wasp is very conspicuous on sandy shores above high-water mark, where the female may frequently be encountered dragging a caterpillar to her burrow. The caterpillar is usually bigger than the wasp, which drags it along under her body, holding it in her jaws.

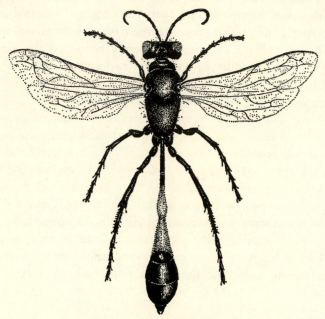

Fig. 14. *Ammophila sabulosa* ($\times 3\frac{1}{2}$)

As long ago as in 1710 the great naturalist John Ray described how he saw one of these wasps dragging a caterpillar three times bigger than itself for a distance of fifteen feet. It is interesting to quote Ray's subsequent observations: '. . . (the caterpillar) was deposited at the entrance of a hole previously dug in the sand. Then, removing a pellet of earth from its mouth, (the wasp) descended into the cavity, and, presently returning, dragged the caterpillar down with it. After staying a while, it again ascended, then rolled pieces of earth into the hole, at intervals scratching the dust into it like a dog with its forefeet, and entering it as if to press down and consolidate the mass . . . Having filled the burrow to a level with the surrounding earth so as to conceal the entrance, it took two fir leaves (i.e., pine-needles) lying at hand, and placed them near the orifice, as if to mark the place. It then flew off.'

Ammophila campestris, though less littoral in habit than the preceding species and more likely to be encountered on inland heaths, is sometimes found in the same habitat as *sabulosa*, from which it may be distinguished by its smaller size. The coloration is similar, but the eyes are black (they are brown in *sabulosa*) and the legs are more spiny.

If all else fails, take a × 10 hand-lens and examine the first segment of the abdomen (which at first sight looks as though it is the hind part of the thorax). At this point there is a shield-shaped plate, known as the *propodeum*. In *campestris* this plate is very finely scored with inverted V-shaped markings; this character is not found in *sabulosa*.

Podalonia hirsuta is confined to sandy places in southern areas. Although actually the same size as *Ammophila campestris*, it is much bigger-looking owing to its more stockily-built body, much shorter pedicel or 'wasp waist' and the dense hairy covering of the black foreparts, giving it a furry appearance; even the basal joints of the antennae are furry as well as the head and face, thorax and the thighs of all the legs. The coloration of the abdomen is the same as in *Ammophila sabulosa* and *campestris*. The male may be distinguished from the female by some silvery hairs on the face and thorax.

We shall now look at some other Sphecids, which comprise by far the largest family of solitary wasps, of which the Ammophilids form only a comparative minority.

CHAPTER VI

Grasshopper and Cricket Predators

THE grasshopper and cricket-hunting Sphecids are not represented in Britain, but are conspicuous in Europe and, more particularly, America. They prefer warm conditions and, if you stop to think about it, you will realise that this is so because their prey is more abundant in warmer climates: it is simply a question of 'where the prey is, there will the predators be gathered together'. Grasshoppers and crickets are essentially tropical and sub-tropical insects, grasshoppers in particular being devotees of warmth and sunshine, and the further north you go the fewer you will find.

One group of the Sphecids feeds upon these insects almost exclusively, nearly all of them following the prevailing custom among Sphecid wasps of first digging the nest and then hunting for the prey with which to provision it. This would certainly seem to be a more logical process to adopt than the reverse arrangement adopted by the Pompilids or spider-hunting wasps, which first catch their spiders and then dig their nests; which, in human terms, would be on a par with first buying all the food and then going out to choose a fridge, leaving the food stocks unattended in the street for anybody to appropriate in your absence. Obviously these wasps' minds run on different lines!

Nesting habits of Sphex

One of the sphecids studied by Fabre in the south of France is the well-known *Sphex flavipennis*. This is a cricket-predator which makes its nest in the bare sand, in colonies. Bear in mind that colonial nest-building bears no relation to the concept of social organisation as adopted by the paper-nest makers; the fact that large numbers of females may make all their burrows in one sandy area merely points to the fact that that particular area is a suitable site, and the wasps might as well use it rather than forage farther afield, where such a good site might not be available.

Getting back to Fabre's French sphecid, the first part of the burrow is horizontal, and the wasp uses this for shelter in inclement weather. The wasp usually builds three cells, though occasionally two, or four, have been recorded. These cells open into a central passage. Fabre has recorded that 'this wasp digs with the rakes on its forelegs, making as it does so a shrill singing noise'. Fabre maintained that he could even hear the 'singing noise' after the wasp had burrowed some way underground. The noise is thought to be a kind of 'Keep Out' warning to other would-be burrowers, and has been noted by other observers, not only in *Sphex* but also in some Ammophilid species.

As in the case with some of the Pompilids or spider-hunters later to be described, there may be several false starts before the final site for the tunnel is decided upon. The so-called Great Golden Digger of America, the black and yellow *Sphex ichneumonea* (Fig. 15),

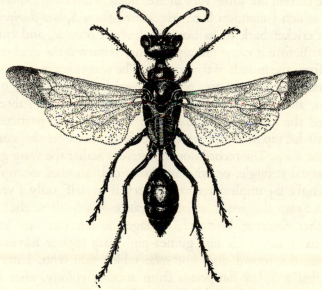

Fig. 15. *Sphex ichneumonea* (×2)

can take anything from fifteen minutes to four hours to dig its burrow, according to the hardness of the soil.

After *Sphex flavipennis* has found and overpowered a cricket, it stings it, first usually in the region corresponding to the 'neck', then again in the abdomen; Fabre took this to mean that the nervous centres of the cricket were thereby paralysed. Usually only female grasshoppers or, more commonly, crickets, are caught by these wasps, as these are larger and more succulent than the males. The wasp then grasps the prey and drags it forward along the ground, and a few have even been observed pulling their victims vertically up a wall. Some stalwarts actually fly with their burdens embraced, as it were, by their legs, and since the prey usually weighs considerably more than the wasp does, the wasp cannot make much height and carries it in short bursts of flight, and when it reaches the nest it lands with a decided belly-flop. The prey is laid down across the nest entrance; the wasp then enters the nest head first, turns round, and goes out again head first, seizes the prey by the antennae and drags it into the burrow by walking in backwards. One cell usually requires to be provisioned with two crickets or grasshoppers.

Fabre carried out some very interesting and amusing experiments, one of which I mention here. He waited for a *Sphex flavipennis* to bring a cricket back to its burrow, leave it outside, and enter the burrow. Before it came out again Fabre removed the cricket a few inches from the mouth of the burrow. The wasp clearly disapproved, for it marched smartly out, pulled the cricket back into its original position, and then went back into its burrow again. Fabre again removed the cricket, with the same result. In one particular experiment he repeated this procedure forty times on the same unfortunate wasp. The record does not state whether the wasp gave up the unequal struggle, or whether Fabre did: another example of a tantalisingly incomplete record. I'd try it myself, only I've never found a *Sphex flavipennis*, either in France or anywhere else!

Another observer, however, managed to last out one hundred and three times with his 'guinea-pig' wasp (*Sphex ichneumonea*), but again the record does not state which side won. Later Fabre found that a *Sphex flavipennis* from another colony, after having been experimented on in this manner three or four times, eventually learned to carry the prey straight into the burrow without leaving it outside at all; the same thing happened with the behaviour of various Sphecids observed by the Peckhams in America.

The observer Reinhard experimented with a black Sphecid wasp found in America, *Sphex pennsylvanica*, which preys upon the long-horned grasshoppers known as 'katydids' in that country. From one to six katydids are used to provision the cells. After provisioning had begun, Reinhard blocked up the entrance holes of three of the nests, so that when the wasps returned with the katydids they could not take them in. They appeared very obviously baffled, and, after flying around for some time with their burdens, they dropped them, and went off to look for more.

Over a period of three days, two hundred and fifty-two paralysed or dead katydids were found outside the blocked-up entrances to the nests. Once more I have to report that the experiment was not fully documented as to its outcome; did the wasps eventually fly off and stop looking for katydids, or did they try to unseal the blocked passages, or even build new nests elsewhere? No one seems to know.

Another American observer studied a wasp known as *Priononyx atratum*, a closely-related species which, unlike *Sphex*, catches its prey before digging the nest-hole. One of these wasps caught a grasshopper, left it on the ground, and commenced its nest-burrowing operations. It appeared very nervous while digging, constantly interrupting its work and going to see whether the prey was still there, each time bringing it a little nearer to the entrance to the burrow by dragging it along the ground. While engaged on these observations, the biologist in question noticed that the wasp was being followed at a respectful distance by a little parasitic fly known as *Metopia leucocephala*. The *Metopia* took no positive action until the burrow was about to be closed; it then dashed in and laid its eggs before the wasp returned to the burrow.

The eggs of *Metopia* hatch almost immediately after laying, which has led some biologists to describe it as 'ovo-viviparous'. Once its own egg has been laid, the wasp closes the mouth of its burrow, hammering the sand down with its head. (This habit is one of the differences between the Sphecids and the Pompilids, which use the end of the abdomen for this purpose). This nest closure is only temporary, sand being scuffed over in a rather rough-and-ready manner, so that it can be easily moved aside again to admit the wasp.

Some species, instead of making a separate cell for each grub, construct one large chamber in which a number of grubs grow up amicably together—at least I hope so—in a sort of wasp-grub commune.

The egg of the Sphecid wasp hatches in up to four days. The first cricket or grasshopper is consumed by the grub in from six to seven days, when it moults, and then starts on its second victim. The grub remains in the larval stage for up to twelve days, frequently less; it then spins a cocoon, the process taking about forty-eight hours. The pupal stage lasts about twenty-four days.

When the adult wasp emerges it stays in the burrow for about three days, during which the outer integument hardens and the pigment develops, so that the wasp, by the time it is ready to chew its way out, is equipped to start a new life in the outside world. It may live as an adult for about two months.

A related genus called *Isodontia*, which make their nests in holes in wood, hollow stems and so on, also provision their nests with crickets or grasshoppers. The nests are lined with fibres from grass or from the bark of trees. Wasps of this genus have been seen snipping off lengths of grass, often several times longer than their own bodies, and flying off with them. The nests are closed with a plug of compacted grass, upon which is laid a section of coiled grass-stems; finally, some blades of grass are arranged longitudinally.

Sphecids are very vulnerable to a number of predators. Besides the *Metopia* flies already mentioned, birds sometimes attack the females as they enter their nests. The Sphecids also have more than their fair share of parasitic predators.

Mention should be made of an African sphecid which hunts the migratory locust. As is well-known, migratory locusts frequently engage in mass movements on a colossal scale, laying waste all vegetation in their path. One observer, C. B. Williams, studying the movement of desert locusts in East Africa, observed that the swarm was accompanied by numbers of a large black wasp, *Sphex aegyptia*. I will now quote from Dr. Williams's report: 'A great swarm of desert locusts began to settle at about 11 a.m., and within fifteen minutes I noticed dozens of a large black Sphecid wasp running about . . . My two assistants caught 168 specimens within an hour, in an area of a few square yards . . . Immediately upon arrival the sphecids began to burrow, and very soon they were dragging paralysed locusts along the ground into their burrows. They continued this all day until dusk, and started again the following day shortly after 7 a.m.'

Dr. Williams goes on to say that between one and two o'clock on the following day the locusts took to flight, and within an hour only four remained of the sphecid wasps which had accompanied them, whereas two hours previously thousands had been counted. Many of them departed so hurriedly that they had left behind hundreds of open half-finished burrows, and paralysed locusts were lying about by the hundred.

An observer six miles away said that he had seen large numbers of 'black bees', flying low down, with a loud buzzing noise; these were obviously the sphecid wasps to which Dr. Williams has referred. One very odd thing is that all these wasps were females, and Dr. Williams wondered whether this species is parthogenetic, especially as this phenomenon is well known among Hymenoptera; there are some species of which only the female sex is known.

It is astonishing that the instinct of the sphecids to follow the swarm of locusts is so powerful that the females even interrupt their instinctive drive to excavate their burrows, provision their nests and lay their eggs. No one has yet come up with a really convincing theory; so far, all we have are various interesting hypotheses.

CHAPTER VII

Fly, Wasp and Bee Predators

THE Sphecids include various groups of wasps which prey upon flies, bees and other wasps, and we shall first look at the genus *Oxybelus*, which includes some of our most interesting solitary wasps. These wasps have a pair of small sharp spines on the hind part of the thorax, which serve to distinguish *Oxybelus* from all other wasps. Most authorities list four species as British, but only three need be described, as one has been taken on only one occasion.

The commonest species, *Oxybelus uniglumis* (Fig. 16), is less than a quarter of an inch in body length, and scarcely recognisable as a wasp to many, who imagine it is a small fly. It has bright silvery bands on the body, and black jaws; this last point is very important as a diagnostic feature, differentiating it from the next species, *Oxybelus sericeatus*, which is distinguished by having very pale-coloured jaws. *Oxybelus uniglumis* may be further distinguished by the banded abdomen, as *O. sericeatus* has a shining black abdomen with a white spot on each side of the first four segments.

In early summer the females may be found digging their burrows. Sometimes they choose a sandy bank, but at other times level ground may be preferred. The burrow, which ends in an oval chamber, is only two or three inches long.

This wasp is among the few which block up the mouth of the burrow before going off hunting. The prey, which consists of various two-winged flies, are caught in flight or while resting on flower-heads. They are carried to the burrow impaled on the sting, an ingenious method of transport used by no other wasp. These wasps are also well known for their great speed in collecting flies; an observer who timed one of these females found that she caught six flies in five minutes. From four to twelve flies are used to provi-

sion each cell. The parasites of these wasps include various sarco-
phagous flies, and also the so-called 'velvet ants' or mutillids, which
are actually wasps (see Chapter X).

Oxybelus argentatus is a little smaller than either of the foregoing,
and can be immediately recognised by its all-over silvery appearance.
In Britain it is, however, restricted to the south coast of England,
where it nests in sand-dunes. A very interesting point is that it
preys on only one particular species of fly, which is also silvery in
appearance like itself, and it is thought that this enables the wasp to
go among them, as it were, unsuspected.

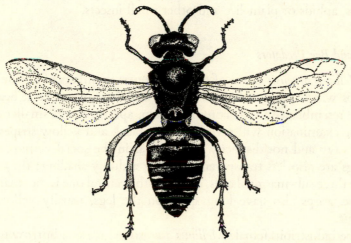

Fig. 16. *Oxybelus uniglumis* (×7)

The genus Crabro

A larger group of wasps have the generic name of *Crabro*, which
would indicate a resemblance to the hornet, but this is rather a
misnomer. These wasps are very much smaller than the hornet and
also do not sting, and most of them are black, though a few are
banded rather obscurely with dull yellow. There are thirty-seven
species on the British list, but some are great rarities. The name
Crabro—which has tended to cause some confusion—was decided
upon by one of the pioneer entomologists of an earlier century; but

for the law of priority, later authorities certainly would have preferred some other name to supersede it.

The habits of the wasps of this group are very varied. Some make holes in the earth; others excavate decaying tree-stumps or rotting logs, while yet others choose the stems of brambles or other plants, hollow reeds, or the straws of thatch. A few species have been seen nesting in nail-holes in old wood, the abandoned tunnels of the wood-boring larvae of other insects, or even in empty oak marble-galls.

Most wasps of the genus *Crabro* prey upon various two-winged flies, but a few of the smaller species prefer gall-midges, fungus-gnats, aphids or plant-lice and other small insects.

Fly and Bee Predators

Mellinus arvensis is one of the commonest members of a group of wasps which prey on bees as well as flies. In appearance it bears a close resemblance to the common wasp, apart from its smaller size. Close examination will reveal that the black and yellow stripes are less wavy and not distinctly separated as in the social vespids. The wings are also less transparent, bearing a dusky shading; they also have three sub-marginal cells, of which the central one is the smallest. These wasps also have long spurs on the legs, usually yellow in colour.

The industrious female *Mellinus arvensis* excavates a burrow up to two feet in depth in bare sandy soil, and the cells, which may number up to ten, lead off from this at various depths. This particular species preys upon various flies to provision her nest, from four to nine being used according to size; the flies are first placed in the cell and the egg is laid on top of the last one. She then closes the individual entrance to each cell from the main shaft.

The female is frequently observed stalking her prey on meadow flower-heads, which are covered with flies on sunny days. She chooses her potential victim, and proceeds to within an inch of it; then she will leap up suddenly and land upon its back, seizing it with her feet and jaws. She then stings it, and thus the quieted victim can be transported to the nest.

Several females of this species may often be found making their burrows in close proximity. This, however, as with other solitary wasps, does not in any way imply social behaviour; it is merely a question of the locality being suitable for nest-building, so the wasps choose it as being more convenient than seeking a site further afield.

The building of the cells, and the provisioning of each in turn as it is completed, take up considerable time, and by the time the last cell is being provisioned the first egg will have already hatched. This has led many of the early observers to suppose that the cells remained open and that the growing larvae were fed with fresh food, but this is not so. The cells are mass-provisioned and the entrance sealed; the wasp is merely carrying on providing for the later arrivals.

Parasites of Mellinus arvensis

Once again, this wasp has its own specific parasites, mainly several species of dipterous flies which appear to be taking their revenge for the numbers of their fellows that the wasps destroy. The female parasites wait outside the burrow entrance, and nip in when the wasp has left on a foraging expedition. The parasites then lay their eggs in those cells which are still open, so the sooner the wasp can manage to block up the entrances to the cells the better it will be for her offspring. When the fly does succeed in laying its egg in the wasp's cell, the larva on hatching first eats the luckless grub and then its store of food.

In the situations favoured by *Mellinus arvensis* the wild carrot and other umbelliferous flower-heads attract many flies. The wasp therefore takes advantage of this and haunts these flower-heads in order to obtain the flies with which to provision its nest.

Bee predators

Another member of this group is known as the 'bee-killer' because it preys upon bees and kills them before taking them to provision its nest. These wasps, known as *Philanthus*, are not very common in Britain, but quite plentiful on the continent of Europe, where their predatory habits are well-known, as many bee-keepers are only too willing to tell you, since *Philanthus* hovers over bee-hives and systematically destroys many honey-bees. It has also been observed forcing bees to disgorge the nectar which they have gathered to feed their broods. The bee-killer wasp is little more than half an inch long, but she does not fear the sting of larger species, and manages to out-sting them every time. The colour of this wasp is bright yellow except the head and thorax, which are black. There are also some triangular black bands across the abdomen.

The nest of *Philanthus* is built in sand, and can be up to three feet deep. From eight to ten cells open out from the foot of the shaft in horizontal series. This wasp is much more careful than some others in this group in blocking her nest-entrance. When she is out hunting she closes the entrance with soil; when she goes home, it is with this same soil that she blocks up the entrance from the inside.

The bee-killer wasp, like her close relatives, has a great many different parasites, not only flies, but also other wasps. Curiously enough, there do not seem to be any species of bees which take their revenge upon *Philanthus*.

Bee and beetle predators

Another sub-group includes the genus *Cerceris*; the six British species all have black and yellow stripes, and the beginner may quite easily identify them as they have a distinctive marking not found in other black-and-yellow wasps. In all these other wasps the sides of the abdomen are curved in a smooth line, but in *Cerceris* species each of the abdominal segments is curved at the sides into a crescent-shape, so that it is broader in the middle than at either end. This gives a kind of 'unfinished' appearance to the abdomen, which is quite distinctive. There is also a more or less distinct 'tail', formed by the two sloping sides coming to a point. These two diagnostic features suffice to identify any *Cerceris* species immediately. Five of the six British species prey upon beetles, while the sixth species is a bee predator.

Cerceris ribensis excavates a small burrow in the ground, only about three inches in length. The end of the burrow is smoothed out into an oval chamber, and the cells lead off from this, up to six or seven in number.

This wasp usually preys upon *Halictus* and *Andrena* bees, which are caught on the wing while gathering pollen. The wasp, awaiting their arrival laden with their spoils at the entrance to their burrows, pounces upon the back of the unfortunate bee, seizing it by the neck and stinging it several times on the underside of the thorax. The wasp then drags the bee to her burrow by the antennae, because the bee is much bigger than the wasp. Once the burrow has been reached, the wasp pounds and kneads the body of the bee in order to break down its outer integument and obtain the honey which it has consumed. The wasp uses this honey for food, and the bee's remains are used as food for the grubs.

Fig. 17. *Cerceris arenaria* (×4)

The next species, *Cerceris arenaria* (Fig. 17) is common on sand-dunes in southern Britain. It is slightly larger than the preceding species. Since this difference is scarcely noticeable in flight, and both are banded with alternate stripes of black and yellow, the two species are frequently confused. A closer examination will reveal that in the male *arenaria* there are some yellow markings on the thorax, which is all black in *ribensis*.

Cerceris arenaria will frequently adopt a burrow which has been abandoned by a bee. The cells are only about three inches below the surface, and each is provisioned with from five to twelve small beetles. Weevils are the more usually selected group, the favourite genera being *Otiorrhynchus* and *Strophosomus*. Sometimes the cells of these wasps have been found to contain twelve weevils all of one species.

Like its congeners, this wasp is beset with many parasitic dipterous flies, some even accompanying the female on her hunting expeditions in order to locate her nest; the flies will then wait patiently outside until the wasp goes on another hunting foray, and will then enter the burrow and lay eggs in the cells. Unfortunately this wasp does not have the foresight to close the cells while she is gone.

Despite its smaller size, *Cerceris quinquefasciata*, the next species, as its specific name implies, is banded with five stripes, as opposed to three or four in the other species of this genus. Nests of this species have been found in hard sandy ground and even excavated in well-trodden paths. The cells are mostly provisioned with weevils, but this wasp has also been observed capturing small beetles of the genus *Meligethes*, which congregate on the flower-heads of scabious.

The fourth species, *Cerceris labiata*, is the only other member of this genus likely to be encountered in Britain. Its habits are not completely known, but it has been found nesting in sandpits and preying upon weevils; other beetles are also sometimes used. The remaining two species have a place in the British list solely by virtue of their having occurred on one or two isolated occasions, probably as accidental imports from Europe. The last records were many years ago.

Cuckoo-wasps or ruby-tails

The next group, known popularly as the cuckoo-wasps or ruby-tailed wasps, all prey upon other wasps or bees. The family name of Chrysididae derives from a Greek word meaning 'golden'. Indeed, these wasps are among the handsomest of all hymenopterous insects, being brilliantly coloured in metallic red, green, blue, purple, bronze and gold.

The commonest European species is *Chrysis ignita*, popularly known as the fire-tail, which, fortunately for the British hymenopterist, is found in Britain. This species has a brilliant metallic blue-green head and thorax, the abdomen being equally resplendent in metallic crimson. It may frequently be seen flying around walls or gateposts looking for the holes made by its victims.

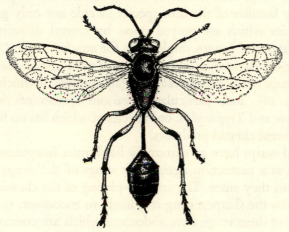

Fig. 18. *Sceliphron spirifex* (×2)

Unlike cuckoo-wasps of other families, chrysid wasps' grubs do not feed on the stores of food with which their hosts' cells have been provisioned, but consume the host wasp or bee grub only. This is understandable in a group of wasps which is partial to both bees and other wasps, because bees provision their cells with honey, nectar and pollen, while wasps provision theirs with insects and spiders. If the chrysid larvae were to consume the host's provisions, it would mean that the chrysid grubs would sometimes be reared on a vegetarian diet and at other times an animal diet, which, of course, they do not do, any more than bee grubs would be reared on anything other than their natural food of honey, nectar and pollen.

Chrysid grubs are very different in appearance from the larvae of other wasps; they are covered with hairs, and they bear antennae, which other wasp grubs do not have. They are also much more active than other wasp grubs, and have more powerfully-developed jaws. In cases where the eggs of the host are laid together in one brood-chamber several chrysid eggs may be deposited, and the one which hatches first destroys all the other chrysid eggs before getting down to work on the host larvae. As many as six chrysid eggs have been recorded in one brood-chamber, but never more than one of them has reached maturity.

Chrysid wasps are cuckoos of a large number of wasps and bees, and many families of the host species include not only genera but even species which are preyed upon by several different chrysid species. Favourite groups singled out for attack include *Osmia* bees (including *Osmia rufohirta* which makes its nests in snail-shells), mud-nesting wasps of the genus *Sceliphron* (an example of which is shown in Figure 18), and, particularly, various species of the genera *Trypargilum* and *Trypoxylon*, one species of which has no fewer than seven different chrysid predators.

Chrysid wasps have an extremely hard outer integument, which is needed as a protection against the stings of the wasps and bees whose nests they enter. The armour-plating of the chrysid is proof against even the sharpest sting it is likely to encounter. In addition, a number of these wasps have abdomens which are concave on the ventral surface; the wasp therefore also has the advantage of being able to bend its head and thorax forward into the abdominal con-cavity, thus rolling itself up into a ball, rather like a hedgehog, and leaving no vulnerable part of its anatomy exposed.

The fly predator Bembix

The genus *Bembix* is an important one with many representatives distributed throughout North America and Europe. Unfortunately for the British hymenopterist, these wasps stop just short of the Channel; the odd one or two have turned up in Jersey, Guernsey and other Channel Islands, but they are not indigenous. This genus affords the best examples among solitary wasps of progressive provisioning.

These wasps, unlike their near relations the *Ammophila* species, are much more stockily-built and superficially bee-like in appearance, with the 'wasp-waist' not much in evidence. They have relatively large heads compared with the size of the body, and large eyes compared with those of wasps of other groups.

Like *Ammophila*, *Bembix* females dig their burrows mostly in sand. Some prefer hard sand, others loose. One American species nests in vertical sandbanks, which are too steep for the wingless 'velvet ants' (see Chapter X) to climb. These creatures are the main predator of this particular *Bembix* species.

Besides the 'velvet ants', the *Bembix* wasps have a great many other predators, especially small flies related to the bluebottle. These follow the example of the parasite of *Ammophila*, which wait around the entrance to the burrow, rush into it as soon as the female leaves on a hunting foray, and rapidly deposit an egg, or even a living larva, in the case of those species which are ovo-viviparous. There are also some other parasites of this group related to the bee-flies (*Bombylius*) and *Anthrax*, which have the peculiar habit of hovering round in the vicinity of the nests and hurling their eggs roughly in the direction of the nest-hole; the young larvae then crawl into the nest when they hatch.

Many nests are usually built together, giving the appearance of a colony, but appearance is as far as it goes for there is no social organisation and each female works only for her own brood. An interesting feature of several Bembix species—seen also in one or two other sub-groups—is the digging of auxiliary burrows. These are usually near the true burrow and left unclosed. A number of theories have been advanced as to their function. One authority considers that they are merely temporary sleeping quarters, while others think that they may be excavated as a 'blind', to entice would-be parasites to lay their eggs in an empty hole and thus avoid finding the real nest-site. An American observer, Evans, photographed one of the 'velvet ants' walking round from one open false burrow to another and in this process actually passing over and ignoring the real nest-burrow, which had been closed and camouflaged.

Some of these wasps, when they finally close the real nest-site, obtain the material used for doing so from another site nearby and thereby excavate another hole in the ground in the process. This, possibly, may have been the origin of these auxiliary burrows, but they have certainly, even if this is so, acquired a secondary purpose, because it has now been proved that they are sometimes made *before* the true burrow is closed.

One species, *Bembix pruinosa*, makes a very elaborate false burrow, which is dug at first parallel to the surface and not very deep down; then, perhaps, after a couple of feet or so, it suddenly makes a steep dive downward for about the same distance, so that eventually the whole false burrow may be as much as five feet in length. The burrow containing the actual nest is then excavated as an offshoot of the lower part of this first burrow, and when a cell has been completed and an egg laid in it, the wasp leaves by another entrance near the point where the burrow began its downward descent.

Progressive provisioning in Bembix

Provisioning is then commenced. A very unusual method of provisioning is adopted by *Bembix pruinosa*. The nest itself opens on to a long, narrow chamber. The wasp brings a number of flies, paralyses them with her sting, and leaves the bodies lying in a row along one wall of the chamber. The grub, when it hatches, progresses along the row devouring the flies one after another, the first one, of course, being the one laid nearest to it so that it consumes the earliest specimen first, leaving the freshest ones till last—a kind of wasp-grub fridge. Evans has referred to this rather amusingly as a 'wasp-larva cafeteria'.

Not content with this elaborate form of provisioning, the female wasp also collects all the débris left behind by the grub and walls it up in another part of the burrow, which is then sealed. A very reasonable theory about this has been put forward: the female wasp's concern is not entirely on the grounds of hygiene but also to discourage predators which, attracted to the nest by the dried legs and wings and other inedible portions of flies, would not only consume the grub's provisions but the grub itself. Evans quite rightly considered that if the female wasp had to keep bringing enough food for her own offspring and for the intruders, she would be kept so busy that she would probably end up provisioning far fewer nests.

Another species, *Bembix u-scripta*, has an odd habit which may be concerned with the frustration of potential predators. As she digs her burrow a mound of earth is raised behind the entrance hole. When the burrow has been completed the wasp proceeds to shovel the mound of earth away from the hole by facing forwards and scraping it back. She ends up with another mound of earth a few inches away from the original site. Near the entrance itself the ground is perfectly level. Wasps of this group vary considerably in the extent to which they carry out these levelling operations.

Bembix u-scripta and other *Bembix* species frequently rest inside their burrows, effecting a temporary closure from the inside. *Bembix sayi*, when she finally closes her nest, packs sand down firmly with the tip of her abdomen and then scrapes a number of paths leading away from the entrance to smooth down the soil. Some American *Bembix* species make only one cell in each burrow, some two, while others make up to five or six.

As we have seen earlier, wasps make orientation flights in order to familiarise themselves with the whereabouts of their nests. Some of the *Bembix* species are very proficient at this, as they fly with their prey from considerable distances and dive with it straight into their burrows. Evans, when experimenting with one of these wasps by moving objects near the nest, found that the wasp was hardly at all disturbed by his so doing. He then stood with one foot over the hole; she just waited until he removed it, and then dived in.

Most *Bembix* species hunt flies. Some are easy to please and will take flies of any family; others are more fussy and prefer particular genera or even species. One will take only tabanids. A European species concentrates on bee-flies (*Bombylius*) and their relatives; this seems a good thing because, since the bee-flies are parasites of both bees and wasps, *Bembix* obtains food for her young and removes potential predators at the same time.

In some cases, where a number of flies are brought in quick succession for provisioning the nest, these are killed instead of merely paralysed, because they do not have to be kept fresh for any length of time as the larvae will shortly consume them. It has been observed that, while earlier provisions may be killed, later ones may be paralysed. It has also been seen, in some cases, that before flies are laid down in the nest ready for larval consumption, a wing or a leg may be removed so that the fly will fit more easily into the space allotted to it.

While the larva is small, only a few flies will be needed; the daily ration is increased as the grub grows. One *Bembix* was observed to collect altogether seventy-nine house-flies, eighty-two other flies and twenty tabanids before its larva spun its cocoon. Another almost fully-fed larva, already starting to spin its cocoon prior to pupation, consumed an additional twenty-six flies when these were offered. The average duration of the larval stage is from seven to ten days in this group.

Adaptation to specific habitats and the conditions demanded by them are seen in certain *Bembix* species, which have on this account departed from orthodox *Bembix* behaviour. One species, *Bembix linei*, which nests on the seashore, finds conditions suitable for it only for limited periods and therefore has to work very quickly; thus it has abandoned the habit of progressive provisioning. Another species, on the other hand, cares for more than one nest at once, rather like *Ammophila* does.

A very strange adaptation has developed in *Bembix u-scripta*, referred to earlier. It hunts flies at dusk when they are at rest. Evans records that although nests were seen to be full of fresh flies, he could never see the wasps actually at work doing the provisioning when he made his afternoon observations. One day, however, he stayed later than usual in the area in which he was making his observations, and he noticed several females provisioning their nests with resting flies which they pounced on in the surrounding vegetation. He also discovered that females emerged again from their nests just before sunset, and on following them he found them apparently engaged upon the same errand. Flies found in the burrows of *Bembix u-scripta* comprised thirty-three different species of nine different families. This wasp has carved out a very special niche for itself ecologically, in which it has absolutely no competitors.

Another smaller species of this group, *Microbembix*, is one of the commonest solitary wasps in North America, where it, too, has carved out an ecological niche for itself practically devoid of competition. It is more catholic in its tastes than any other known solitary wasp, preying on insects of at least ten different orders. It even collects dead or helpless insects or even portions of the bodies of dead insects. It cruises around looking for food for its offspring, picking up various items here and there and rejecting what is found to be unsuitable. Items collected include spiders both living and dead, the legs of grasshoppers, dead as well as living beetles, bugs, flies, moths, caterpillars and ants. A very curious thing is that the wasp has not lost its instinct to sting the prey, because even when there is no need to do this she still observes the instinctive routine of stinging all her captures, however dead and however unsuitable they may be. Apart from this habit, its other habits are very similar to those of the more orthodox members of the *Bembix* family, carrying its prey between the middle pair of legs, laying its egg in an empty cell, practising progressive provisioning, and making several auxiliary burrows in which it sleeps.

As we have seen, wasps of this family are in many ways similar to the ammophilids. Both show a great diversity of habits and, in particular, one may observe in both these sub-groups the first signs of progress towards the social organisation which is seen so clearly in *Polistes*, *Polybia* and other social vespids.

CHAPTER VIII

Bug, Cicada and Hopper Predators

A GOOD many sub-groups of Sphecid wasps prey upon bugs, which common term includes stink-bugs, assassin-bugs, shield-bugs or Pentatomids and other plant-bugs of various kinds, as well as cicadas, leaf-hoppers and frog-hoppers. There is insufficient space to deal specifically in detail with all of them, so we shall look at a few representative genera and species from these groups.

A genus of bug predators, the majority of which are black-and-red in colour like the shield-bugs on which they prey, are known as *Astata*, the vast majority of which are American species, although two, *Astata boops* and *A. stigma*, are found in Britain, where they prey upon the nymphs of various shield-bugs. The word *Astata* means 'restless', which exactly describes their behaviour, especially that of the males, which have the habit of perching on flowers or stones, sometimes for hours at a time, but breaking the continuity by frequent short excursions into the air, flying up and down and back again. Frequently they will also walk about on the stone or flower-head before coming back again to their original position.

The nests of *Astata* species are very often excavated in very hard soil, and the main burrow usually has several ancillary side branches leading to the cells, which may be arranged in series. The nests of *Astata* are very hard to find, as they are usually camouflaged under the shelter of drooping foliage. The prey of *Astata* is usually the soft-bodied nymphs of pentatomid bugs of several different species, many of which are not merely paralysed but stung to death.

Astata has a distinctive habit shared by very few other wasps. Not only does the female make orientation flights around the nest when leaving for the hunt, but when she approaches the nest to bring back her prey she will do so in a roundabout manner, obviously to confuse potential enemies. The prey is grasped around the middle with the legs, while she secures additional purchase upon it by gripping its antennae in her jaws. As the nest is approached she will fly down to the ground and drag the victim along and into the mouth of the burrow. As with *Philanthus* and her bee victims, a number of bug carcases are temporarily stored before being finally distributed among the various cells.

The egg of *Astata* is laid on the underside of the victim's body, not on the upperside, as with *Philanthus*. These bugs have very tough outer integuments, so the larva of *Astata* on hatching must be able to find a vulnerable spot on the under-surface at which to commence feeding.

Fig. 19. *Sphecius speciosus* ($\times 1\frac{1}{4}$)

Turning now to the cicada-predators, the chief of these is undoubtedly *Sphecius speciosus* (Fig. 19). This is an American species, and a very large and handsome one at that, rusty red in colour on head and thorax, and striped on the abdomen with black and yellow, with russet-coloured wings. There is one other species of this genus found in Southern Europe, but it is nothing like as conspicuous.

Sphecius has the task of transporting a very bulky object for its prey: the cicada is, perhaps, more awkward to carry than heavy. The wasp hooks its middle pair of legs under the wings of the cicada and carries it belly upwards. It has to climb up to a certain height, such as up the stem of a plant, in order to gain height for a successful take-off. An amusing instance is recorded in the American literature of one of these wasps which climbed up the observer's trouser-leg for this purpose. The cicada being a large and succulent creature, two are normally sufficient to provision the cell for each *Sphecius* grub, if it is a queen-cell, while the smaller male grub usually makes do with only one.

Another sub-group which preys upon small plant-bugs, aphids being one of their favourite objects of prey, are the very slender black-and-red wasps of the genus *Psenulus*, which, in their shiny uniform of smart stripes, look rather like miniature versions of *Ammophila*. They nest in burrows in wood or plant-stems or in straws, and store large numbers of aphids—up to thirty-six in one cell have been counted. These little wasps are very industrious, and frequently continue working after sunset.

Another related sub-group, *Mimesa*, consist mainly of sand-burrowers; many of their holes are usually found close together. A few *Mimesa* species, however, nest in wood. These wasps are often seen flying back and forth across bushes, apparently aimlessly to the casual onlooker, but are in actual fact looking for leaf-hoppers. One observer discovered that fourteen out of nineteen hoppers of one species which were captured by one of these wasps had already been attacked by an internal parasite, which was the larva of another kind of wasp; this had possibly made their movements sluggish, so that they were more easily caught. A few *Mimesa* species affect littoral habitats and are partial to sand-dunes; one recently-discovered species is known only from two areas of sand-dunes on the Irish coast.

Some of the smaller plant-bugs are the prey of other sphecids such as the black-and-yellow striped *Gorytes*, which specialise in frog-hoppers (*Cercopidae*). From ten to fifteen frog-hoppers are required to provision one cell, and *Gorytes* then closes the nest by pounding soil into the entrance with the end of the abdomen, just as the Pompilids do.

Several of these frog-hopper predators are found in Europe. One species, *Gorytes mystaceus*, is one of the commonest solitary wasps found in Britain. As is well known, the immature forms, or nymphs, of frog-hoppers are familiar as the producers of the so-called 'cuckoo-spit' found on grass and other low plants. The 'spit' consists of water and waste products of the nymph, whipped up into a froth which serves to protect the soft-bodied nymph sitting inside. This protection may be very good against some predators, but it is no deterrent to the *Gorytes* wasp, which plunges head first into the froth and drags out the luckless nymph. At least, that is the way—according to one observer—in which *Gorytes* works; but, according to another observer, it stays outside the froth, merely inserting its legs to drag out the nymph, and then stings it before carrying it off. There is room here for some additional research. It is quite possible, of course, that individual *Gorytes* wasps may, possibly, use either method, or even a third method which has not yet been observed or described.

Another species of this group, *Gorytes campestris*, differs from the majority by not closing the mouth of the burrow when leaving it. The burrow extends downwards for about four inches, and then turns at right angles to form a horizontal chamber, also about four inches in length. From six to nine cells are made, each of which is provisioned with about 20 or more frog-hoppers. Unfortunately for the *Gorytes* young, one of the Chrysids or ruby-tailed wasps has ample opportunity to enter and lay her eggs in the partly provisioned cells of the unclosed nest, so that eventually when the eggs in the *Gorytes* nest hatch into grubs and pupate, the wrong kind of wasps come from them.

CHAPTER IX

Beetle Predators

A NUMBER of wasps prey upon beetles, more particularly on beetle grubs, and we shall now look briefly at some of these, firstly at the wasps of the family Tiphidae. Two of these are found in Britain; the larger of the two is a littoral species, while the smaller one is found inland. The adults frequently visit the flowers of wild carrot and other umbelliferous plants and their habits are similar to those of Scoliids. In some cases *Tiphia* wasps do not kill the beetle grub outright but merely paralyse it to a slight extent with the sting—in fact to such a slight extent that the beetle grub quickly recovers and carries on feeding while the *Tiphia* larva which hatches from the egg laid by the wasp feeds on it. The smaller of the two species, *Tiphia minuta*, preys upon *Aphodius* or dung-beetles, while the larger one, *Tiphia femorata*, is a predator of chafers (*Melolonthidae*).

It must strike the reader that the wings of those wasps which prey upon underground beetle grubs must be rather a hindrance to them if they have to burrow down underground to hunt their prey. Nature has provided for this eventuality very ingeniously by making the females of many of these wasps wingless, although the males are winged. The wingless females, as will be seen from the figure of the European *Methoca ichneumonioides* (Fig. 20), look very ant-like.

Methoca ichneumonioides, which, as its name implies, bears a superficial resemblance to an ichneumon, is a predator of the larvae of tiger beetles, or *Cicindelidae*. It is the only British representative of the family *Methocidae*, and is by no means a common insect, rather the reverse.

Both the larva and the adult of these beetles are predaceous. The larva lives in a burrow, sometimes a foot deep, in sandy soil. It stations itself at the mouth of the burrow, blocks the entrance with its head and thorax, and waits for some unwary insect to come within range, when it is quickly snapped up.

The *Methoca* wasp female, which is black-and-red striped and very slender, wanders around just under the surface of the soil until she finds the burrow of one of these tiger larvae; she slips inside, and stings the larva under the 'neck'. Usually she has no difficulty in doing this, but at other times the tiger larva may seize her in its jaws. This is when her flexible abdomen comes into its own, as she can bend it in any direction and sting the unfortunate tiger grub at some vulnerable point on its body. Some observers have seen quite long fights ensue between *Methoca* wasps and tiger grubs, until the latter eventually become paralysed.

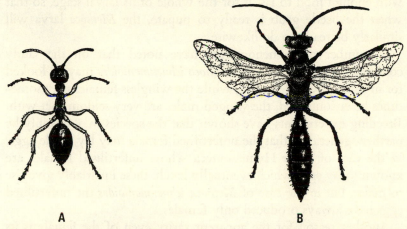

A   **B**

Fig. 20. (A)Wingless female of *Methoca ichneumonioides* (B)Winged male (both ×4)

After stinging her victim, *Methoca* retreats to the top of the burrow, and here displays a very interesting trait, because she waits for ten minutes or so to allow the poison injected by the sting time to take effect, and then she cautiously descends to examine the tiger grub to see whether the sting has taken effect. If so, she administers a few more stings for good measure, and then lays her egg upon its body. The *Methoca* female then withdraws from the burrow and closes it.

It may be asked how we can know such a lot about these underground activities. Several observers have kept tiger beetle larvae in glass jars of sand, covered by cardboard or brown paper, so that when the latter is removed one side of the burrow can be seen against the glass, and therefore available for inspection, when the activities of a subsequently-introduced *Methoca* female may be watched and recorded (see Appendix I).

One of these observers, H. T. Pagden, has recorded that a *Methoca* female may occasionally pass the night in the burrow of a tiger grub without attacking it. In his report Pagden states that he was unable to see why the grub was ignored. It is possible that the beetle larva was at the wrong stage of development for the *Methoca* to use it as a pabulum for her young. The beetle grub must be at a stage to allow sufficient time to grow, in order to supply the *Methoca* larva with enough food to last it for the whole of its larval stage, so that when the beetle grub is ready to pupate, the *Methoca* larva will similarly be ready to do likewise.

A number of hymenopterists have noted that on the sandy commons where the British *Methoca ichneumonioides* may be looked for in June, July and August, while the wingless females may sometimes be encountered, the winged males are very seldom met with. Breeding experiments have shown that the species may possibly be parthenogenetic, so that the unfertilised female may lay fertile eggs. In the case of other Hymenoptera whose unfertilised females are known to lay eggs which eventually hatch, these invariably give rise to males, but in the case of *Methoca ichneumonioides* the unfertilised eggs have always produced only females.

Another reason for the apparent rarity even of the female is its great similarity to an ant, which could cause it to be overlooked, especially by the beginner and the less experienced hymenopterist.

CHAPTER X

The Mutillids or Velvet Ants

In the last chapter we saw how *Methoca ichneumonioides* and some other allied species have wingless females. In the next family, the *Mutillidae*, commonly known as 'velvet ants', all the species have wingless females. These wasps are very small, and have a velvety appearance, which, together with their ant-like shape, has given rise to their popular name.

In Britain there are only two species, one about twice the size of the other. The larger one is parasitic upon humble-bees, especially *Bombus agrorum* and *B. humilis*. Despite the fact that it is rather local in occurrence, occasionally it is so successful that the nest of a *Bombus* may yield more velvet ants than humble-bees.

Even the inexperienced hymenopterist is unlikely to mistake the wingless female of the larger species, *Mutilla europaea*, as it is quite distinct from any other related insect and identifiable at sight. The female, when taken, should be compared with any ant such as *Formica rufa* or *F. fusca*, when the differences will be at once apparent.

Female Mutillids are much commoner than the males—probably for the same reason as in *Methoca*—though as far as the two British species are concerned, 'common' is not the best word to describe either sex. The female *Mutilla europaea* is red-and-black in colour, with distinct abdominal stripes, and is about half an inch long, all parts being entirely clothed with downy hairs, even to the antennae and legs, which are black. The head and thorax are deeply pitted. The two compound eyes are small, and there are no simple eyes (*ocelli*).

The winged male may be looked for on the blossoms of bramble and other plants. The wings are dark, and the eyes much larger than those of his mate. The abdominal coloration, too, is quite different, as it is a deep blue with silvery-white fringes.

The female of the smaller species, *Mutilla* (or *Smicromyrme*) *rufipes*, is somewhat similar in coloration to that of the preceding species, except that the antennae and legs are reddish, hence the specific name (*rufipes* = red-legged). The thorax is also red. The male of this species is more like the female in appearance, except for a few fine silver fringes along the edges of the abdominal segments, but these are discernible only through a hand-lens, and in any case are easily worn off by friction against vegetation in older specimens. This species is decidedly littoral in habit and affects sandy heaths near the seashore as well as dunes on the shore itself.

As we have seen, *Mutilla europaea* preys upon the larvae of two *Bombus* species. The egg is inserted into the body of the bee grub, which is then eaten parasitically by the *Mutilla* larva. On emerging from the cocoon the males leave the *Bombus* nest, but females remain there for some time after emergence consuming the bees' honey-stores, in order to obtain protein and other nutrients essential to fertility.

The smaller of the British velvet ants preys upon Sphecid wasps; while there does not, apparently, seem to be any particular preference, the only sphecids which have been noted as its victims are the smaller species which excavate burrows in sandy situations.

Although not technically Mutillids, the closely-related wasps of the family *Myrmosidae*, which also have wingless females, are also sometimes referred to as 'velvet ants'. Their only British representative is very ant-like in form. This wasp, which rejoices in the name of *Myrmosa melanocephala*, is a denizen of heaths and sand-flats where it preys upon sphecid wasps such as *Oxybelus uniglumis* and various *Crabro* species. K. G. Blair in 1926 discovered this wasp entering the burrows of *Crabro elongatula* and established its association as a predator of that species.

In the female the head and thorax are black and shining and the antennae brick-red, darker at the tips. The abdomen is brick-red, delicately fringed, with some segments lighter and some darker, giving a striped appearance, and the legs are also brick-red.

The male is so different in appearance that the novice is hardly likely to imagine it to be the same species. It is entirely black with a fine covering of silvery hairs, and black nervures in the smoky wings. The possession of wings makes it look much larger than its actual size, which is little more than a quarter of an inch in total length.

When looking for the females of these wasps, it is as well to be a little cautious in handling them, as they have an extremely long and efficacious sting, which, despite their small size, can give repeated painful stabs. In tropical countries the powerful stings of mutillid wasps and their close relatives have earned them such popular names as 'cow-killers', 'mule-stingers' and the like. These exotic species often possess brilliant orange or red bands or large spots, which would seem to be warning colours, as the wingless females are very conspicuous as they wander about looking for the nests of their victims. The winged males are usually much more sombre in hue, and, of course, do not sting.

The mutillids are well-distributed on the southern part of the European continent and in the U.S.A. as well as in the tropics, and are very troublesome to other Hymenoptera, upon which they are parasitic. Like the Chrysids, they have a hard outer integument, which is not readily pierced by the defensive stings of their enemies. Some are strictly host-specific, but others are much more catholic in their tastes and may prey upon either wasps or bees. The main wasp groups attacked by them include the genera *Crabro*, *Oxybelus* and *Bembix*. As with Chrysids, the female mutillids lay their eggs on fully-grown resting larvae. They may be seen crawling around on the ground looking for the nests of their potential victims. They then burrow down, break open the cell wall and bite through the cocoon in order to lay an egg.

Krombein studied some of the species which entered the trap nests which he had prepared specially to attract them. He noticed that normally they attacked only the outermost cell of a linear series. After opening the cell and the cocoon and laying their eggs, some Mutillids went so far as to seal up breaches in the cocoon, but they failed to do the same with the partitions between cells, and so there was very little to prevent other parasites from getting in later. Some of them did not even bother to seal up the outer entrance to the cell. On the other hand, at least one female mutillid wasp has been observed, before laying her egg, to make a thorough inspection, apparently to ensure that other parasites had not got in before her.

Female *Rhyssa persuasoria* × 1¾

Worker of Common wasp
(*Vespula vulgaris*) with sting
extended

Queen Common Wasp $\times 1\frac{1}{2}$
(*Vespula vulgaris*)

Common Wasp (*Vespula vulgaris*) -
interior of nest showing comb,
capped cells, larvae and newly-
emerged adults.

Dead caterpillar of Scarce Vapourer
moth (*Orgyia gonostigma*) and
Apanteles larvae $\times 1\frac{3}{4}$

Larva of a large ichneumon–wasp
inside pupa of Eyed Hawk-moth
(*Smerinthus ocellatus*)

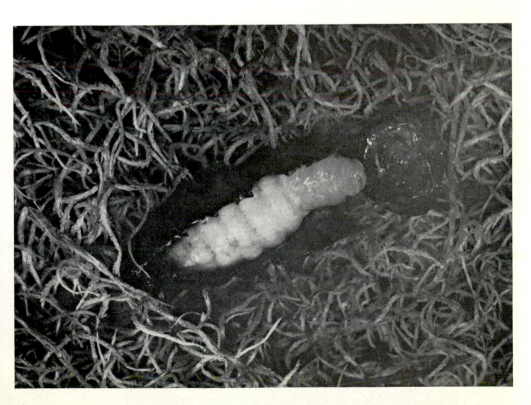

Female Ichneumon-wasp (*Amblyjoppa proteus*) ×1½, bred from caterpillar of Large Elephant Hawkmoth (*Deilephila elpenor*)

Female Yellow Ophion (*Ophion luteus*)

Female Sand-wasp (*Sphex sabulosa*) and her victim, a large Sawfly larva

Queen Hornet. Head enlarged

'Coin-gall' or 'Silk-button gall'
(*Neuroterus numismatis*) on oak

'Oak-apple' (*Biorrhiza terminalis*)

Oak marble gall (*Cynips kollari*)

Rose bedeguar gall or 'robin's pincushion' (*Rhodites rosae*) on wild rose

CHAPTER XI

Solitary Wasps: The Potters and Masons

ALL solitary wasps are hole-nesters or burrowers except the potters and masons. Most other wasps make their nests in the ground, or in decaying wood; a few extract pith from plant stems and build cells in the tubes thus formed, one above the other, rather like a high-rise block of flats. The potters, which we shall look at first, make vase-like pots of mud or sand—sometimes minute pebbles are incorporated into the raw materials—moulding them with water into exquisite shapes and attaching them to woody plant-stems, or, less commonly, to wooden posts or beams.

All solitary wasps, as well as solitary bees, provision their cells. Wasps are carnivorous; in this respect they differ markedly from bees, which use only nectar, pollen and honey. Wasps feed their larvae on insects or spiders, which have first been paralysed with the sting, in order to keep them alive without any danger of decomposition, until such time as the developing larva is ready to consume them.

Most wasps are highly selective in their choice of prey. Spiders, caterpillars, weevils, flies of various kinds, bees and other wasps, grasshoppers and crickets, bugs, aphids or plant-lice, froghoppers and their nymphs from 'cuckoo-spit'—all these are preyed upon relentlessly by various wasps, but the predator of one particular type of invertebrate will not hunt those used as food by another group. Thus, a spider-hunter will not use caterpillars to feed to its larvae, and vice versa. It is possible, in theory, that the type of venom from the sting of one particular species, or group of species, has no effect on the type of victim selected by another group; but this is only conjecture.

Eumenes and other potters

The potter wasps, as well as the masons, are related to the social vespids, which include the common wasp, the German wasp and the hornet. Unlike these latter, the potters and masons are all solitary species. The genus *Eumenes* is typical of the potters; *Eumenes* wasps also have a special characteristic not shared by other sub-groups: when at rest they fold their wings longitudinally, which no other wasps do.

Nest-building in Eumenes

A typical species of potter wasp is the European *Eumenes coarctata*, which is the only *Eumenes* species found in Britain. It is reasonably common in heathery and sandy places, where the female may be seen building her nest of mud, making a very beautiful little pot shaped like a Grecian urn. These miniature flasks are fixed to the stems of heather or, more rarely, to other low plants; they bear a superficial resemblance to the bell-flowers of *Erica* species and even their colour is similar, thus heightening the resemblance.

The pot is built of mud, made from earth or sand brought in the jaws and water-droplets similarly carried, which are then pounded together to the right consistency, and formed into a hollow sphere. The mouth of the sphere opens into an expanded neck, so that the whole pot is flask-shaped.

The *Eumenes* female builds several of these pots, frequently adjacent. The neck of the flask, although expanded beyond the actual opening, is still too narrow to admit the female; all she can do is to insert the end of her abdomen, with ovipositor extruded, into the pot to lay her egg, one in each pot.

Before laying her eggs, the female *Eumenes* goes off to find the caterpillars she requires to provision the cells. She collects only small smooth green caterpillars which can be pushed through the very small entrance hole in the narrow neck of the pot; she cannot enter herself, so she just pushes the caterpillars through. How does she know when she has brought enough caterpillars? No one but *Eumenes* herself, guided by unerring instinct, knows the answer.

Each pot contains only one cell, where the larva is raised in splendid isolation. About twelve green caterpillars are required to stock one cell and provide for the whole of the larval stage.

The egg is suspended from the roof of the cell by a thread-like filament hanging just above the store of caterpillars. The female seals the entrance, leaving her offspring surrounded by enough food to last it till pupation.

After sealing the entrance, the female then busies herself building another pot. The pots are sometimes, though not always, built in close proximity, but it must be remembered that this in no way constitutes social behaviour, merely the convenience of the female in building. The young larvae, and the wasps that eventually develop from them, never have any contact; they do not normally even hatch simultaneously, since the eggs are laid one at a time, each egg-laying involving several trips for provisioning and the sealing of the cell before the female builds her next cell and lays her next egg.

On hatching, the larva eats the first caterpillar while still attached to its eggshell suspended from the roof. It then drops on to the remainder of the store, and eventually manages to get through them all before pupating. Finally the adult wasp emerges, chews its way out of the pot, finds a mate, and so the life-cycle starts all over again.

Eumenes are the only wasps to suspend their eggs by a thread from the cell roof; all other wasps lay direct on the paralysed bodies of the prey. When the egg hatches, the grub takes its time in coming out of the eggshell; it does not leave it immediately, as most wasp grubs do, but sits with its hind end in the eggshell and reaches out to pick up the first caterpillar and to eat it. During this process the larva grows, gradually coming further out of the eggshell, and the young grub, when it has completed its meal, sometimes withdraws into the eggshell, until after a day or two it has grown enough to make it too big to do this, so that it cannot get back again.

Eumenes wasps are noted for not being very thorough in stinging their caterpillar prey. In a good many cases the caterpillars have recovered, and even escaped. Fabre conjectures that the object of the suspensory thread of the egg was to preserve the young hatchling larva from possibly being crushed by wriggling caterpillars which had overcome the paralysing effect of the sting.

Fabre tried to rear *Eumenes* larvae by using methods which had been successful in his experiments with other wasps, but he never succeeded in rearing any *Eumenes* species. He attributed this to the fact that the thread from which the egg is suspended in nature was unable to be reproduced under artificial laboratory conditions.

When the adult wasps finally emerge from the cocoons, they usually rest for a day or two before breaking down the cells in order to harden the outer integument.

The Eumenid wasps prey mainly upon geometrid moth larvae or 'loopers', though a few species specialise in leaf-mining micro-lepidoptera, cutting open the mines to sting the caterpillars before extracting them and carrying them off to their nests.

The food habits of most European and North American Eumenids are more orthodox, but the construction of their nests shows a wide range of originality. Sometimes a female *Eumenes* will incorporate little bits of quartz in the mud, flint or even tiny snail-shells. Decorative pottery was being made long before the time of man!

The mason wasps

Of the fifteen *Odynerus* species occurring in Britain, several are great rarities, having been taken only once or twice. Most are small in size, with yellow-and-black abdominal stripes.

The specific name of *Odynerus spinipes*—*spinipes* means 'spiny-legged'—is rather misleading, for spines are found only on the femora of the middle pair of legs in the male, and are absent altogether in the female. The so-called 'wasp-waist' is not very well pronounced, as the pedicel is extremely short. The abdomen has a highly-polished appearance.

The nest is usually a burrow in the face of a bank of earth or sand, but sometimes the female will use the soft mortar of a wall that requires repointing. *Odynerus* species are capable of boring into even the hardest materials; this ability has been noted by all observers of solitary wasps since the days of Réaumur. Apparently a softening fluid is produced from the mouthparts which breaks down the materials to enable the mandibles to penetrate them.

In the case of earth-nesters, the boring is excavated vertically downwards for a few inches; at the bottom of the shaft three or four branches are usually mined. The material dug out is brought up to the surface in the jaws, and built into a turret-like structure at the mouth of the burrow. Some species construct very elaborate tubular entrances, sometimes vertical, sometimes turning down at an angle. Some of these tubes may be several inches long. The object of these tubes is a matter of speculation. Are they built to help the wasp recognise her home, by being built in a special way, or are they intended to confuse intending predators? The latter theory strikes me as being more likely. There is opportunity here for someone to observe, experiment and find out!

The female *Odynerus* then lays one egg in each of the cells, which are situated in the branches at the bottom of the shaft. The eggs are suspended from the roof of the cell, rather like those of *Eumenes*. *Odynerus* then proceeds to mass-provision each cell with about twenty or more small caterpillars, which will suffice the grub for its entire larval development. The caterpillars chosen as prey run through a very wide range of species, though small smooth green ones are preferred by the majority, especially by the smaller species. The larger wasps choose victims with a bit more body to them. Some hunt only nocturnal-feeding caterpillars; these latter hide at the foot of their foodplant in the day time, and it is during the hours of day light that the wasps find them, probably by scent. One large species of this group supplies only one very large caterpillar to each cell, dragging it along the ground. A number of species of this group are highly host-specific, confining their attentions to only one species.

When all the cells have been provisioned, the female *Odynerus* then proceeds to demolish the turret at the entrance to the burrow, carrying the soil or sand down in her jaws and blocking the interior entrance to the nest. No predator can then gain access, and without the external turrets the nests also look far less conspicuous.

An African member of this group, *Odynerus vespiformis*, frequently takes drops of water to the abandoned empty mud nests of other species to break down the materials from which they are made and re-fashion these into her own nests. She also sometimes uses tenanted nests for her materials, and in such cases will eat the grubs in the other species' nests or, more rarely, take them home to feed her own

grubs. Some members of this genus also practise progressive provisioning, and a tropical Old World genus, *Stenogaster*, cares for
several nests simultaneously. These two habits are steps in the direction of social behaviour (referred to by some authorities as 'sub-
social behaviour'), which is taken still further by wasps of the genus
Synagris, one species of which feeds her grubs daily on pre-chewed
caterpillars, while another species also feeds her grubs daily, but
departs from the norm for this group by using as food chewed-up
midges which have been previously snatched out of the webs of
spiders.

An interesting habit is found among some species in the Middle
East, where there are many stones with hieroglyphic writings on
them. Mason wasps have often been seen filling in the depressions
in the stones which form the hieroglyphic writings with mud and
making their cells in them, thereby obliterating the writings on the
stones. This is very interesting to the hymenopterist, but somewhat
disconcerting for the archaeologist. . . .

Another species, *Odynerus parietum*, prefers walls, window-
frames and various nooks and crannies in houses for her nesting-site.
If mortar has fallen out of the brickwork and has not been repointed,
she will usually choose this situation, but instead of levelling off the
mortar like a human bricklayer, she will make a nest which projects
beyond the brick, as some less experienced human bricklayers
have also on occasion been known to do.... On account of her
preference for this kind of situation, *Odynerus parietum* is sometimes
called the 'wall mason wasp'.

In a brick wall the cells are made inside the mortar, but if the
nest is made elsewhere such as in a window-frame, *Odynerus* brings
mud in her jaws, and the cells are built end to end horizontally.
If there is enough space, ten or more cells will be built in one line.
Each cell contains one egg, and is mass-provisioned with enough
caterpillars to last the grub during its whole larval development.
The number of caterpillars brought by one female to provision her
nest includes a very large proportion of the destructive species
which are so harmful to the gardener's choice plants.

Another species, *Odynerus melanocephalus*, burrows in the ground,
also building a small chimney-like structure for additional protec-

tion. It is rather similar to O. *spinipes* in appearance, but the central tooth of the three femoral spines on the middle legs of the male *melanocephalus* is more sharply-pointed, which is not evident in *spinipes*.

The remaining species in this group are so uncommon that they are rarely likely to be met with in the field, so I will not attempt to describe them here. Some of them, however, have been seen making their nests in nail-holes in old posts and other situations, which will give some indication of their diminutive size.

Predators of Odynerus

A Chrysid species, the beautiful little ruby-tailed wasp (*Chrysis viridula*) is the main predator of *Odynerus*. A female will sit patiently outside the entrance to the burrow, waiting for an opportunity to dash past the rightful occupant when she is not looking and enter the nest. If she succeeds, she will lay her own eggs in the cells, and the luckless *Odynerus* grubs, when they hatch, will provide the ruby-tail wasp larvae with a living cafeteria, after which the ruby-tail grubs proceed to dispose of the food which *Odynerus* had so carefully provided for her young.

CHAPTER XII

The Pompilids: Spider Predators

THE Pompilids, or Pompilidae, take their name from the typical genus of the group (*Pompilus*), and they form a very large family of wasps which are very well represented all over the Northern Hemisphere; there are fewer of them in the tropics.

All Pompilids provision their nests with spiders, so they have acquired the popular name of 'spider-hunters'. They are not the only wasps to provision their nests with spiders, but it so happens that this particular group are strictly spider-predators.

The Pompilids are typically very slender in build; most are very small, although there are a few larger species. Their very long legs are frequently furnished with long bristles or spurs, or comb-like structures which are used in raking earth or sand when excavating their burrows. Most are sand-burrowers, building their nests in sandbanks, sand-dunes and similar situations, and many of them are strictly littoral.

The Pompilids are very excitable, as wasps go, and are frequently seen rushing and darting about and quivering their wings in an agitated manner, turning from side to side at the same time. Very few other wasps behave in this way, but this group is particularly noted for behaving in this manner, as though they were acutely conscious of the fact that time was short and they have to get on with what they are doing—which is usually looking for prey to feed the young.

This group has four particular characteristic habits apart from the above-mentioned behaviour and the fact that their only prey is spiders. There are one or two exceptions, but these will be mentioned as they occur. (1) One spider only is used to provision each individual cell. (2) The paralysed spider is transported in the wasp's jaws and dragged backwards along the ground underneath the wasp's body. (3) The wasp uses the end of the abdomen as a battering-ram for pounding earth or sand to close the entrance to the nest; this is the only group that does this. (4) The Pompilids are almost the only wasps which catch their prey *before* building the nest. After catching the prey and paralysing it with the sting, they leave it in a secluded place, or somewhere where they hope they can find it again—there have been recorded many instances of wasps which could not remember where they had put it—and they then excavate the burrow and hopefully go back to find the spider to take into the nest in readiness for the larva when it hatches from the egg.

Prey specialisation in Pompilids

Some Pompilids specialise on one particular species of spider; others have more catholic tastes and accept spiders from various groups. The European species *Anoplius fuscus* accepts spiders from five different groups. A lot depends on how the wasps have been going about their hunting, i.e., which species they turn up. If they are actually looking for a spider which has specialised habits, then the wasps will be adapted accordingly and will also have specialised habits and will tend to limit themselves to spiders to whose habits they are already adapted.

A good many Pompilids can walk about on spiders' webs without becoming entangled. Other species, whose feet are obviously not so adapted, buzz around the web and angrily threaten and terrify the spider until it falls out of the web on to the ground; they then give it the *coup de grâce*. With those species which prey upon the funnel-web spiders we have a rather different situation; it must be quite a fearsome problem for a wasp to enter the lair of a spider which is a funnel-web maker such as a *Segestria* species, or a trap-door spider, when the occupant is facing outwards with poison fangs at the ready. In a good many cases the spider is greatly superior in size to the wasp. There is an interesting record in the literature of a *Pompilus vagans* which attacked a ground-nesting spider which had two separate entrance and exit holes to its burrow. The wasp went into one entrance for a short distance and then ran out again; then it ran into the second one, and again ran out. The wasp then entered and left the first one again, repeated three or four times. This absolutely terrified the spider, which, despite the fact that it was more than ten times the size of the little Pompilid, was so confused and upset by the wasp's tactics that it ran out in a panic, when the wasp immediately jumped on it.

In Fabre we can read about rather similar tactics on the part of *Pompilus apicatus* which attacked a large *Segestria* spider which lived at the bottom of a funnel-web. The wasp and the spider both kept popping in and out of the funnel threatening each other; then the Pompilid would catch the spider by one leg and let it go, then catch it by another leg and let it go, until the spider was absolutely petrified. The wasp now decided to do something more drastic. She grabbed the spider, dragged her out bodily and dropped her on the ground; the spider curled up into a tight ball. This is one of *Segestria*'s defence weapons and very effective against some of its predators, but quite useless against *Pompilus*, which stung it and carried it off to its burrow. The wasp is almost always the victor in these contests, even when the prey is considerably larger, or armed with biting mouthparts or poison fangs; but with sheer agility and tactical superiority the wasp comes out on top.

Sometimes a Pompilid wasp will adopt the burrow of the spider which she has just stung, which saves her the trouble of making a burrow herself. The female leaves the spider in the burrow, lays an egg on its body, closes up the entrance and goes off to look for another spider. One American species specialises in trap-door spiders, and the wasp lives in the burrow with the trap door, just like the trap-door spider. A person looking for trap-door spiders who puts his hand in one of their burrows is frequently likely to be rewarded with a wasp sting—and the Pompilids are noted for the sharp stabbing quality of their sting.

Many species of Pompilids which habitually nest in the burrows of trap-door spiders have lost the combs on the legs which other sand-burrowers in this group possess. During the course of evolution this has obviously gone hand-in-hand with the adaptation of the wasp to use the burrow of the trap-door spider, so that it would not need to have combs to rake or scrape earth or sand to close the entrance; with a trap-door already available to make a firm closure, it does not need to. This is a very good example of a species being adapted specifically for a situation already in prior existence.

These 'trap-door wasps' are very interesting. There is a European genus called *Homonotus* which specialises in a spider which, although not strictly a trap-door spider, spins together leaves to make a nest. The wasp attacks and stings the spider, and lays her egg on the spider's body, but the spider recovers and carries on as usual, apparently oblivious of the fact that there is a wasp's egg stuck to its abdomen. Eventually the egg hatches and the larva starts literally to eat the spider alive, and is in fact a very good example of a parasite, as it first subsists on the skin, fat and other parts of the spider's body, leaving till last the vital organs which keep it alive, so that it will last as long as possible as a food supply, after which it consumes the viscera and thus kills the unfortunate victim. By this time the wasp larva is ready to pupate and start the life-cycle all over again.

Effects of the sting

In all aculeates the sting has been evolved as a modification of the ovipositor or egg-laying tube. This implies that the sting is possessed only by the female, which is, of course, the case. No male wasp has a sting.

When the sting is used the poison is injected from two poison sacs at its base just inside the rear end of the body. In some cases this produces a light temporary paralysis in the victim, in other cases a profound one from which the victim will not recover but will die in a kind of prolonged coma. This, of course, leaves it in good condition as food for the larva.

Earlier in this book I have referred to progressive provisioning, in which comatose larvae are stored in the cell of the larva of the wasp, which thus has fresh food always available in the 'fridge', as it were. Observations have been made by Peckham and others in America as to how long paralysed spiders have taken to recover when removed from nests. Some were already dead, while others survived up to forty days. It appears to vary mainly according to the species of spider concerned and which species of wasp was using it as its prey. A few wasps chew off the legs of the spider, which makes it easier to transport. The few which have been observed to do so were invariably Pompilids. Sometimes a wasp will be a bit greedy and instead of storing the spider for her offspring she will eat it herself; she then finds that she has to go out and catch another one for her offspring. This behaviour, I suspect, is more individual than specifically characteristic. It has not been observed very frequently, but it has been recorded not only in Pompilids but apparently in one or two other groups besides.

The spider is usually paralysed by a single sting inflicted on the underside of the body. The narrow waist of wasps has undoubtedly evolved specifically to enable the abdomen to be curved round underneath the victim so that the sting can be applied in the most efficious place to paralyse the prey, which is on the vulnerable ventral surface.

Transport of prey

We have already discussed the way in which Pompilids drag their prey backwards along the ground to the nest. Observations have also been kept to discover exactly whereabouts on the body of the spider the wasp grasps it in its jaws to drag it along. A few grasp the palps or mouthparts, others the spinnerets, but the vast majority have been observed to hold the spider by the base of the hind legs. Whichever part of the spider's body is grasped, it is still not a very satisfactory method of progress, because the wasp cannot see where she is going, without stopping to look round.

Some Pompilids have improved on this. The wasps of the genus *Dipogon* typically walk sideways with a crab-like motion, so they can at least get a partial forward view. Others walk forwards but intermittently, so that they can stop and look round in the process of transporting the prey.

Prey storage prior to provisioning

The Pompilid habit of hunting the prey before nest-building is fraught with difficulties. One must wonder why the wasps of this group have not gradually gone over to the reverse habit during the course of evolution; there are all too many enemies ready and waiting to grab the unguarded prey, including other Pompilids. The large black-and-red banded *Anoplius fuscus* is one of the chief offenders. Another species, *Anoplius infuscatus*, even goes so far as to keep a sharp lookout for other Pompilids dragging their spiders to their nests; after waiting for the provisioner to close the nest and leave, *Anoplius* will open up the nest and remove the spider, covering it up temporarily with sand, leaves or other débris while she digs a new burrow for it. Again, one is bound to wonder why *Anoplius* does not adopt the other wasp's burrow containing the spider; there seems to be no reasonable explanation for this.

Ants are a great hazard, especially in the tropics. *Pompilus quinquenotatus* climbs a low shrub with her spider and parks it in a convenient crotch while she gets on with her digging, but this does not always prevent ants from reaching it. *Pompilus plumbeus* digs a shallow grave for her spider and covers it with a thin layer of soil while she is engaged in her digging operations.

Many Pompilids interrupt their digging to go back to see that their spiders are still there, sometimes doing this several times. If ants have interfered with them, they are usually abandoned; this may be because formic acid has rendered them unpalatable. Observers have noted how some Pompilids, after going to check up on their spiders, are then unable to find their nests again, and rush blindly here and there in obvious bewilderment. Pompilids do not have to return to their nests once provisioning has been completed, so they have not needed to learn to be good navigators like those wasps which practise progressive provisioning.

Of the forty Pompilids on the British list, the British hymen-opterist may expect to find only a few species at all commonly. Inland, sandy heaths, and on the seashore stretches of sand-dunes covered with marram-grass, are the best places to look for them; where they occur they immediately attract attention with their restless behaviour and feverish activity. While females will be most easily seen scrabbling madly in the sand, the males are best searched for on flower-heads, where they drowse in the hot sunshine supremely oblivious of their mates' preoccupations. Most Pompilids are

either all black, or black with reddish abdominal bands; in some
species these latter are narrow and inconspicuous.

Pompilids are much more numerous in other parts of the world,
where the spiders are bigger and more abundant. A few other wasps
also prey upon spiders, such as the American *Sphex funebris* (Fig. 21),
but this wasp, unlike the Pompilids, first excavates its nest before
hunting for prey, as well as differing from them in many other
ways. The fact that both prey upon spiders is almost the only
behavioural link which the small number of spider-predatory
Sphecids have with *Pompilus* and her allies.

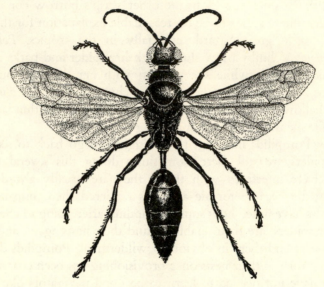

Fig. 21. *Sphex funebris* (×2)

CHAPTER XIII

The Ichneumons

THE ichneumon wasps are frequently referred to in various books as 'ichneumon flies', but this is very misleading, since ichneumons are four-winged hymenopterous insects, whereas the true flies have only two wings and belong to an entirely different and unrelated order of insects, the Diptera.

The ichneumons, together with the gall-wasps, chalcids and braconids, make up the division known as Hymenoptera-Parasitica, as opposed to the Hymenoptera-Aculeata or stinging wasps, bees and ants. The parasitic Hymenoptera have no sting, the ovipositor being used purely as an egg-laying organ.

The ichneumon wasps form a very large group of small-sized insects, though there are some notable exceptions which attain a wing-span of 20 mm. The group ranges across the world, but even the number of British species is so enormous that one particular work devoted to them runs into five volumes. They are fairly easily distinguished from other parasitic Hymenoptera by the fact that the wings are much more veined than the wings of chalcids, braconids and gall-wasps, being covered by a network of nervures forming many cells; the number and position of these cells assist in identifying the genera and species. The pronotum is attached to the centre of the thorax and extends along the sides to the base of the wings; this is another distinguishing feature.

The abdominal segments are clearly-defined, and in the female the ovipositor is short and stout in some species, while in others it may be very long and slender. The modification of this organ is dictated by the requirements of where the egg is to be placed; some species lay their eggs on the skins of their caterpillar victims, but more often the latter is pierced and the egg laid in or under the skin.

In a few cases the ovipositor has to penetrate hard wood in order to reach the larvae of wood-boring insects, or the burrow in which the intended victim is situated.

A larva parasitised by an ichneumon is doomed at the outset, for all its body fluids, fat and eventually even the vital organs will be consumed by the parasite so that it has no chance of survival into the adult stage, although a very few do manage to make it to pupation. In this latter case the ichneumon grubs usually themselves pupate in or around the pupal integument of the hapless victim.

Over twelve hundred ichneumons are found in Britain alone, and one of the largest is *Rhyssa persuasoria*. This species is a parasite of the horntail or greater woodwasp (*Sirex gigas*), and to find it you will have to examine carefully any pine trees which have been bored into by the larvae of the horntail, which tunnels in the solid wood beneath the bark, often at some distance below the surface. How the female ichneumon locates it is not yet fully understood, and to look at its delicate slender ovipositor, which appears quite inadequate for the purpose, you will never believe that this can pierce such hard wood, going right through the bark and into the cambium layer.

The female sometimes deposits her eggs upon the body of the horntail larva, at other times in its burrow. The total body length is about a quarter of an inch, but the ovipositor adds another three and a half inches. The ovipositor is surrounded by two protective guards or sheaths, and many observers have thought that these are used to protect and stiffen it when boring, but this is not so; the slender ovipositor only is used to bore through the wood.

The length of the life-cycle of *Rhyssa persuasoria* is not known for certain, because while the horntail grub spends two years in the wood of the pine tree, it could quite easily become host to more than one ichneumon parasite consecutively (though not simultaneously, as the ichneumon female never parasitises a grub which has already been parasitised by another female). Most hymenopterists do not subscribe to the view that the ichneumon larva also has a two-year life-cycle, and there is room for research here.

Another of our largest ichneumons is a very common species known as *Ophion luteus*, commonly known as the 'yellow ophion' on account of its coloration. The head and body together measure an inch in length, excluding the ovipositor, which is very short and thick and may be observed as a small projection from the end of the abdomen. The entire insect is a dull yellowish-brown in colour. It sometimes flies into houses, attracted by the electric lights, or may be seen fluttering at a lighted shop window in the dark. Despite the lack of abdominal stripes, it has a distinctly waspish appearance, which is emphasised by its narrow waist and pointed abdomen. The abdomen is laterally compressed, so that when viewed from above it looks very thin, but seen from the side it appears very broad.

The yellow ophion is not fussy in its choice of victim. It is partial to the caterpillars of a great many species of moths, including the puss moth (*Cerura vinula*), the broom moth (*Ceramica pisi*), the sycamore moth (*Apatele aceris*) and other noctuids. One caterpillar affords sufficient food for one parasitic ichneumon larva, which, by the time it is fully-grown, has consumed the entire body of its host, leaving only the empty skin. It then spins its own cocoon.

The lepidopterist who breeds moths has a great advantage over the one who does not, in that he can relate the species of ichneumons emerging from his parasitised larvae to the particular species of the host. Much as he may be disappointed that the larvae did not produce the desired moth species, he has a good opportunity of discovering more about the relationships between the various moth larvae and their specific ichneumon parasites, and it is well within the bounds of possibility that he may discover some hitherto unknown facts. Accurate notes should always be kept when breeding moth larvae which turn out to produce ichneumons. If it is possible to preserve the empty larval skins of the hosts alongside the set examples of the ichneumons which emerged from them, with full information about the dates of emergences, foodplant of the host larvae, and so on, it may well prove to add a very useful contribution to our knowledge of these insects.

The life-histories of many ichneumons are completely unknown; in some cases even the host species is unknown. One eminent authority has gone so far as to say that probably a far greater number remain unknown than otherwise, and it is the breeder of moths who has the greatest opportunity of supplying the missing links in our knowledge. Understandably, many lepidopterists are so annoyed at finding their best specimens parasitised by ichneumons that they destroy the evidence of their annoyance without further ado.

Another frequently encountered ichneumon is known as *Paniscus virgatus*, which is something like the yellow ophion in appearance but is smaller and much more slender. The head and thorax and antennae are black; there are some black stripes on the legs and also on the terminal segments of the abdomen, the remainder of which is yellow. Apart from these obvious differences, this ichneumon is remarkably similar to the yellow ophion in general appearance.

Another member of the same group is *Perispudus fascialis* (Fig. 22). This species has a rather curious feature for which no satisfactory explanation has yet been forthcoming: the long and slender antennae of the males have a broad white stripe half-way from the base, which, when the insect is in flight, gives the appearance of broken antennae.

A number of males frequently fly together for long periods around some low bush or tree, although no female has been observed to be attracting them. A possible explanation could be the imminent emergence of a female and they are awaiting this event, but this has not been conclusively proved. The species is easily distinguished from all others by this 'broken' appearance of the antennae, which has been remarked upon by many observers. Similar behaviour has been recorded by K. G. Blair in the males of another species, *Lissonota errabunda*, which he observed flying up and down the trunk of an oak tree for a prolonged period.

The parasitised larvae of noctuid moths frequently produce an ichneumon known as *Ichneumon amatorius*. This, again, is a very distinctive species; over half an inch long, it is black, with a bright yellow 'collar' at the junction of the head and thorax, two yellow bands across the abdomen, and a bright yellow spot on the hind part of the thorax just before it joins the abdomen. It also has conspicuous black-and-yellow striped legs and long black antennae. This insect is frequently confused by the novice with Pompilid wasps, especially when it has been seen emerging from a sand-dune where its victim had buried itself for pupation. It also has no visible ovipositor, which heightens the resemblance even more. However, no Pompilid wasp has a yellow spot on the thorax, so this character alone is sufficient to distinguish it; if you are still in any doubt, you will soon know if it is a Pompilid by the sharp sting!

Another closely-related species is *Amblyteles uniguttatus*, which is not unlike the preceding, apart from the fact that it has no yellow markings; instead, a broad red band goes right round the second and third segments of the abdomen. This species also emerges from sand-dunes, as it preys upon the littoral species of noctuid moths such as

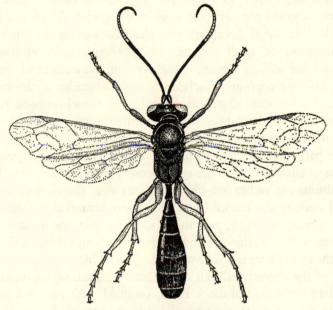

Fig. 22. *Perispudaus fascialis* (×4)

the coast dart (*Euxoa cursoria*), the sand dart (*Agrotis ripae*) and others. Unfortunately for the lepidopterist, the two noctuid moths mentioned are never very common at the best of times. . . .

The drinker moth (*Odonestis potatoria*) is frequently parasitised by another member of the same genus, *Amblyteles subsericans*.

Another ichneumon, *Lissonota setosa*, parasitises the goat moth (*Cossus cossus*), and is about three-quarters of an inch long excluding the antennae. The ovipositor is about 1½ inches long; this length is needed because the goat moth larva lives in rotten wood and, like the larva of the horntail, its burrow is situated some distance below the surface of the bark, though, unlike the horntail which bores in living trees, the goat moth prefers decaying wood. A smaller species, *Lissonota sulphurifera*, has an even longer ovipositor than *setosa*, and parasitises the wood-feeding larvae of clearwing moths (*Sesiidae*).

One particular genus of ichneumons, *Pezomachus*, is noteworthy for the fact that the females are wingless. These females prey upon spiders, laying their eggs inside the egg-cocoons of their host. The ichneumon grubs consume the eggs of the spider, which last them through their larval development. The ichneumons do not attack the immature or adult spiders. The spiders usually chosen are *Drassodes* and *Zelotes* species, which lay large numbers of eggs in flat round egg-cocoons attached to the undersides of rocks and stones. It is obvious, therefore, that the female ichneumon would only be hindered by wings when crawling around under rocks or stones to find the egg-cocoons of the spiders.

One particular species in this group, *Pezomachus aquisgranensis*, cuts a neat circular hole in the egg-cocoons of *Zelotes latreillei*. These ichneumons are rather ant-like in appearance, the distinct slender pedicel making the resemblance even more remarkable. The body is only 4 mm. in length, plus an additional 3 mm. for the antennae, which are yellow at the base and black from about a third of the way up to the tips. There is a yellowish-red band which extends over the whole of the thorax and half of the first abdominal segment; the other half has a central black band, outlined with two red stripes. The second and third abdominal segments are black and the remainder of the abdomen yellow, and the ovipositor is prominent.

One of our rarer ichneumons, *Agriotypus armatus*, is well-known for its peculiar habit of entering the water in order to lay its egg in a caddis-fly larva. It is certainly curious that a species with such an aquatic habit should have a winged female, as she can scarcely use them under water. After the ichneumon grub has eaten the caddis-worm, it spins its cocoon in the empty caddis-case and completes its development under water.

CHAPTER XIV

The Chalcids and Braconids

OWING to the vast number of species and their extremely small size, it is impossible to give a more than general idea of the habits of the two sub-groups of the Hymenoptera-Parasitica known as chaclid and braconid wasps. Those of the chalcids which are familiar to the naturalist generally make themselves so by their attacks upon other insects, much in the same way as the ichneumons attack the larvae of butterflies and moths which are bred and studied by the lepidopterist.

The first thing to be noticed in chalcids is that their wings are much clearer and devoid of venation than those of other wasps. This helps to distinguish them from the braconid wasps and the smaller ichneumons, with which they are sometimes confused.

These parasitic wasps, minute as they are, are in turn parasitised by still smaller species (known as *hyper-parasites*) whose mission in life is apparently to control their numbers. As though this were not enough, these hyper-parasites may in their turn be attacked by other still smaller parasitic Hymenoptera, these being termed *parasitoids*.

As far as the braconids are concerned, the larvae of all the known species live in or on the bodies of other insects, mostly in their larval stages. They do not normally attack the vital organs, but suck the blood and other body fluids.

As a familiar example we may look at the larva of the large cabbage white butterfly (*Pieris brassicae*), which is parasitised by the tiny black braconid wasp *Apanteles glomeratus*. The wasp may frequently be observed in the kitchen garden flying round its intended victim. Despite the movements of the caterpillar in an attempt to dislodge the irritating parasite, the wasp, undeterred, inserts from fifteen to thirty or more eggs into its skin.

In due course the eggs hatch and the minute larvae become evenly distributed throughout the caterpillar's body, mostly in the spaces where blood circulates and where they can feed on the body-fat. When they are ready to pupate they burrow through the sides of the unfortunate caterpillar's body, which is now little more than an empty skin and cannot recover from the inroads of its attackers. The parasites now weave their bright yellow cocoons without moving from the spot, and in due course emerge as a new generation of wasps to help the gardener wage war upon the caterpillars which destroy his brassica crops. These braconids are sometimes referred to by lepidopterists as 'ichneumons', but, although they share with the ichneumons the habit of parasitising butterfly and moth larvae, they are not actually members of that group.

As adult braconids emerge from the skins of parasitised larvae, they usually look round first for healthy, nearly fully-grown specimens nearby of the same brood, which happen to have been fortuitously overlooked the previous autumn, to commence their destructive work all over again.

Chalcids and braconids attack not only lepidopterous larvae but some species are also parasitic upon aphids. One species, *Aphidius*, is in turn attacked by another chalcid, which inserts its ovipositor through the body of the aphis and into the skin of the chalcid larva feeding inside its host.

A braconid, *Praon*, does not mature within the host's body, as *Aphidius* does, but leaves the host while still in the larval stage, and pupates outside the host's body. This braconid also has a chalcid hyper-parasite, *Pachycrepis*.

The larva of the gold-tail moth (*Porthesia similis*) is attacked by the braconid *Microgaster connexus*, which, although less than an eighth of an inch long, is undeterred by its host's urticating hairs. If hibernated caterpillars are dissected in the spring, many will be found to contain anything up to sixty larvae of this braconid parasite. Immediately prior to pupation they bore through the skin of the host and pupate outside the now dead body. This is when they become very vulnerable to various hyper-parasites which lay their eggs inside the cocoons, to be followed by parasitoids which lay their eggs inside the larvae which hatch from the hyper-parasite's eggs; even in the pupal stage there is no escape from the ever-watchful predators.

CHAPTER XV

The Gall-wasps

THE familiar—and some not-so-familiar—galls so often to be found on the leaves, stems, twigs and even the roots of various plants are frequently the result of the activities of certain hymenopterous insects, the cynipids or gall-wasps. Although the various groups of insects responsible for galls are usually termed gall-makers, this title is, strictly speaking, a misnomer, as the insects do not actually *make* the galls, in the sense that a mud-nesting wasp, for example, actually *makes* its nest from the available raw materials. They should more correctly be termed gall-*causers*, since they cause the plant to form the gall.

Galls have been known and written about from earliest times, but still very little is known about them. The Ancient Greeks and Roman used them to dye materials and in tanning hides; their uses have been recorded as far back as 378 B.C.

Not all gall-causers are wasps. Gall-producers include aphids, mites, moths, beetles, dipterous or two-winged flies and midges; even fungi—which of course are plants—are responsible for certain gall formations. Cynipid wasps, however, form a very large proportion of the gall-causing insects, although their exact numbers are uncertain, since many of their life-histories are little-known, or even, in a good many cases, completely unknown. Even the life-history of *Cynips kollari*, the common oak marble gall-wasp, which is probably the commonest gall-wasp in Britain, is imperfectly known. Certain gall-wasps—of which *Cynips kollari* is an example—have two alternating generations, in which two different plant hosts are used and the gall which appears in the second plant is different from that produced in the first, and for many years entomologists thought they were caused by two different species of gall-wasp.

In Britain alone there must certainly be very many species of gall-wasps still awaiting discovery, as well as chalcids, braconids and other small species which are easily overlooked even by the dedicated hymenopterist. When you come to think of it, it must have taken someone with very sharp eyes indeed to discover the somewhat curiously-named *Alaptus magnanimus* which, at ·21 mm. or considerably less than one-hundredth of an inch in length, is the smallest-known insect in the world. It is a parasitic gall-wasp, and it lays its eggs inside the eggs of other insects which are themselves practically microscopic. I think I am pretty safe in assuming that there may well be others around which are even smaller, only their sheer invisibility having excluded them from the attentions of hymenopterists.

We should now take a closer look at gall-formation. One gall-causer, the saw-fly which causes the red bean gall, injects a drop of fluid into the leaf-tissue as the egg is laid. This fluid acts as an irritant and causes the leaf-tissue to swell up; the gall is fully formed by the time the egg hatches. This is almost the only gall whose formation is known without doubt; the gall will still develop, even if the egg is destroyed.

Although some kind of secretion undoubtedly triggers off gall-formation, it cannot in a good many cases be a fluid secreted by the female at the time of egg-laying, as the gall does not begin to form until after the larva has hatched. If the egg is destroyed, the gall will not form. Theoretically there are a number of ways in which a larva could secrete an irritant substance into the surrounding plant tissues; it could secrete such a substance from a special gland, or it could secrete it internally and pass it out of the body during excretion of wastes. It could even 'breathe' the substance out in the form of a gas. No one really knows very much about this process, which is likely to differ in various families, genera, or even species. In fact the whole area of gall-formation is a virtually unexplored territory, and a vast field of discovery awaits the research entomologist who has a good microscope and a vast and unlimited amount of patience.

What we do know more about—at least up to a point—is which species make which galls, so that we are at least able to recognise the species which has been at work by its gall (assuming that it is a known species and a known gall). One plant can bear a fantastic variety of galls; this alone points to the fact that galls are non-host-specific and the plant of itself does not make the gall, otherwise all the galls on one plant would be alike. It also implies that the various species of gall-causers active on one plant have individual gall-causing secretions or other methods of producing the gall.

For example, in the three commonest galls found on the oak—the oak-apple, the oak marble-gall and the oak spangle-gall—it has not been possible to separate the (presumably) three different secretions (if any) which have caused galls of such widely-differing appearance on the same plant. The assumption is that whatever it is that causes the formation of the gall affects the cambium layer, or growth cells of the plant. In a great many species the egg does not hatch until several months after it was laid, and only then does the gall start to form. If the egg is infertile or for some other reason fails to hatch, the gall does not form.

The saw-fly earlier referred to actually lays its eggs in the cambium layer—if the egg is not laid in the correct layer then it does not hatch and no gall formation takes place. The cambium layer consists of actively-dividing growth cells, so it could also be conjectured that the hatching of the egg and/or the subsequent activities of the larva release some kind of hormone into these growth cells which distorts them, affects their mitotic division or in some other way affects them and causes the gall to form.

Many cynipids, especially those which affect oak, display the phenomenon known as *alternation of generations*. In the first year there are two broods, the first, known as the *unisexual generation*, producing females only, and the second (the *bisexual generation*) producing individuals of both sexes. The females of this second generation hibernate to survive the winter and then produce the all-female spring generation. These spring generation females are so different in appearance from females of the summer brood that they were formerly thought to be a different species, and even experts named them accordingly. Even their galls are different in a great many instances (though not always) and may arise on different parts of the same plant (though again, not always).

Let us look at the common oak-apple as an example. In January if you care to dig at the roots of oak you will find the hard brown spherical root-galls (the generic name of the gall-wasp which causes this gall is *Biorrhiza*, which means 'root-life') and these galls always produce wingless females, which bore through the hard outer wall of the gall, burrow up through the soil and crawl up the trunk of the tree and into the branches, exposed to the elements and to predators such as birds. Eventually, if they make it without mishap, they gain the extreme tips of the twigs, where they lay their eggs in the terminal buds.

Adler observed one female to lay 582 eggs in two buds over a period of eighty-seven hours. Sometimes, as may well be imagined, the attack is too much for the bud; the tissues are destroyed under the relentless onslaught of the sharp ovipositor, and no gall appears. But if *Biorrhiza* does not allow herself to be carried away by her reproductive fervour, when the buds begin to swell in May the galls form rapidly; the 'oak-apple' appears within about two weeks, and is mature by the end of the month. The rosy colour (hence 'apple') appears, and if at this stage one cuts open the gall one will see a number of cells or chambers, in each of which a *Biorrhiza* larva is usually snugly esconced, plus its inquilines, parasites, hyperparasites and parasitoids (which we will deal with later).

The *Biorrhiza* grub matures in July and chews its way out through the outer wall of the gall; the little round exit holes must be familiar to everybody who has ever collected natural history objects on a country walk, even in primary school. Both males and females emerge, the females wingless, or occasionally with rudimentary wings useless for flight. Mating takes place at the end of July; the fertilised females crawl down the trunk, burrow in the soil down to the roots, pierce these with their ovipositors and lay their eggs, and the life-cycle of *Biorrhiza* begins all over again.

Biorrhiza is typical of all two-generation gall-wasps, in that all the unisexual spring generation live out their early stages in soft galls of rapid growth, while the bisexual summer generation are associated with hard protective galls of slow growth to see them through the encroaching frosts of the ensuing winter.

The all-female generation of gall-wasps would appear to be parthenogenetic; in laboratory experiments no males have ever been bred out. How and why parthenogenesis actually occurs no one has yet ever been able to find out. Parthenogenesis occurs in certain insects only; all other forms of animal life require the participation of both male and female to produce new individuals.

As a curious opposite example I will briefly mention the goose-berry saw-fly, which in its unisexual generation produces males only by parthenogenesis. If unfertilised females from the bisexual generation are kept separately they lay eggs which produce males only, but if the females are fertilised, their fertile eggs produce only females! Curious indeed—and nobody knows why—not even the experts.

In the case of *Cynips kollari*, the oak marble gall-wasp, females only emerge from the marble galls. Thousands have been bred out in laboratories and no male has ever been seen. It is still uncertain whether *Andricus*, a gall-wasp which produces smaller marble galls on turkey oak, is in fact the bisexual generation of *Cynips kollari*. This theory has some adherents, mainly based on the fact that in 1897 Beijerinck placed virgin females of *Cynips kollari* on turkey oak, watched them oviposit in the buds, and took the buds into the laboratory, where they were kept under observation under strictly controlled laboratory conditions. Male and female *Andricus* emerged, but Beijerinck failed to get them to oviposit on ordinary oak. Others have tried it since, invariably with the same result. I have tried it, but my *Andricus* females would not oviposit at all on anything. Why don't *you* have a go?

The oak marble gall-wasp is the easiest gall-wasp to breed out, unlike *Rhodites rosae*, the rose bedeguar gall-wasp, for instance, which needs the living plant before it will produce its galls (this species always appeals to beginners first owing to the attractiveness of the 'ragged robin', 'robin's pincushion' or rose bedeguar gall). From December onwards the oak marble galls of *Cynips kollari* may be collected. Reject all which have a hole in them; those galls with a small hole *Cynips* has left voluntarily, while those with larger holes indicate that *Cynips* has been forcibly evicted by birds, together with his—or rather her—inquilines, parasites, hyperparasites and parasitoids, of which more anon. Only whole galls are worth collect-ing, and those fallen to the ground are usually untenanted. I could tell you that where the hole has been bored neatly to the centre the culprit was a woodpecker or a nuthatch; where the gall wall has been bashed in, a coal tit or other allied species was responsible; and so on. But this is a book about wasps, not birds. . . .

Do not remove the galls from the twigs. Stand the twigs upright in a tall container with their lower ends held firmly in damp silver sand. The open top of the container must be very tightly covered with muslin of the finest mesh available, and even then some of the smaller of the practically microscopic hyperparasites will manage to do a flit. Still, presumably it is the gall-wasps themselves you are more interested in, especially if you are going to see what you can make of the *Cynips kollari/Andricus* syndrome. Spray the twigs with fine rain-water spray once a week. Even if you don't make some wonderful discovery about the *Cynips kollari/Andricus* relationship, you may quite possibly discover yet another new species of inquiline, parasite, hyperparasite or parasitoid of oak gall-wasps.

Some interesting galls to look for in Britain include the following:

Neuroterus quercus-baccarum (Oak spangle-gall). The undersides of large leaves may bear anything up to three hundred of these small discoid galls, which have raised centres and are clothed with purplish-brown hairs. These galls may be collected from July to October, and in that or the preceding month they become detached from the leaves and fall to the ground, where the larvae complete their development.

In about March of the following year the parthenogenetic spring generation of females emerge to lay their eggs among the young foliage. Males and females of the resulting bisexual generation emerge from these much smaller galls in June, and the fertilised females lay their eggs in the undersides of the leaves, piercing the epidermis with their ovipositors, to give rise in due course to the all-female 'spring generation' which produce the spangle-galls.

Neuroterus numismatis (Coin-gall or silk-button gall). This is another species affecting the undersides of oak leaves, from June onwards, but instead of a raised central boss they have depressed centres. They are also much smaller than the galls made by the preceding species—

so much so, in fact, that over twelve hundred have been counted on a single leaf. The galls are reddish-brown in colour and covered with silky hairs.

The larval development takes the same course as in *Neuroterus quercus-baccarum*, the emerging adults laying their eggs in the young leaf-buds in the following spring. These develop pale green galls which give rise to the bisexual generation of gall-wasps, which emerge in June, and it is the fertilised eggs of these which give rise to the 'coin-galls' above described. Both generations are heavily parasitised, especially the 'coin-gall' generation.

Cynips scutellaris (Cherry-gall). This is so called from its rosy-pink spherical appearance. A few galls only are attached to the midrib and main veins on the underside of oak leaves. Very occasionally a gall will appear on the upper side.

The adults emerge in late autumn, and deposit their eggs on the dormant winter buds. The resulting spring generation produce galls of a completely different appearance, quite devoid of the attractive bright colour of the autumn galls; they are very small, ovoid in shape and dark violet in colour. The spring generation emerge at about the end of May, and start the production of the autumn 'cherry-gall' generation.

Andricus fecundatrix (Artichoke or Hop Gall). This gall is not found on artichokes or hops but on oak; the name merely refers to a fancied resemblance of the galls to artichoke-heads or hop-cones. Inside the external protective scales the actual gall is concealed. When larval development is well under way the gall becomes detached by wind, and falls to the ground.

The imago emerges the following spring, although occasionally emergence may be delayed for two or even three years; no explanation has yet been forthcoming for this. The adults which emerge from these galls are invariably parthenogenetic females, which produce the alternating bisexual generation of hairy catkin-like galls. These mature in May or June.

Rhodites rosae (Rose Bedeguar or Robin's Pincushion Gall). This is a very attractive gall, very popular with students. The female gall-wasp lays a large number of eggs in one terminal shoot bud of the rose, both wild and cultivated, and the gall so caused produces a number of long slender green filaments, resembling a tuft of moss, which later becomes brilliant crimson in colour. Some of these 'robins' pincushions' can be as much as two inches in diameter.

A cross-section of the gall at this stage will reveal numerous larvae, each in a separate cell or chamber. In addition, numerous inquilines, parasites, hyperparasites and parasitoids will probably be found, frequently actually feeding on the body of the *Rhodites* grub. Some will be other gall-wasps and ichneumons, but the smallest ones are likely to be chalcids.

One of the cynipoid inquilines, *Periclistus*, is an exception to the rule in gall-wasps in that it does not cause a gall but deposits its eggs in the existing bedeguar gall tissues. Its larva is in turn parasitised by a chalcid, *Eurytoma*, which works its way systematically through all the cells occupied by inquilines.

Several parasites, both ichneumonid and chalcid, lay their eggs not only in the larvae of the primary gall-causer but also in those of the inquilines. These parasites are in their turn attacked by hyper-parasites such as the chalcid *Habrocytus bedeguaris* and its near relative *H. periclisti*. The mossy outgrowths of the bedeguar gall are there-fore quite ineffectual in preventing the ingress of parasites and predators.

It is interesting to observe that these chalcids never lay their eggs in the *Rhodites* larvae, only in the inquilines. When you come to think about it, this is little short of a miracle, considering that these female chalcids cannot even see what they are doing but just drive their ovipositors into the gall through the outer wall, yet they have never been known to lay their eggs in the 'wrong' species.

Very few galls, even the smaller ones, still remain tenanted only by the primary gall-causer by the time they are mature; most con-tain a number of 'uninvited guests'. These confer no benefit on the host but are tolerated (as opposed to true symbiotics which confer a certain degree of mutual benefit upon each other). Each gall therefore supports a whole association or complex of different in-sects, which are not all necessarily gall-wasps, or even Hymenoptera.

Liposthenus latreillei (no common name) (Fig. 23). This is one of the comparatively few gall-wasps colonising herbaceous plants other than Compositae; in this case the plant colonised is the ground ivy (*Glechoma hederacea*). The gall is spherical, greenish at first, turning red at maturity. One larva only inhabits each individual gall. The larva pupates in August or September, but the imago does not emerge until the following May.

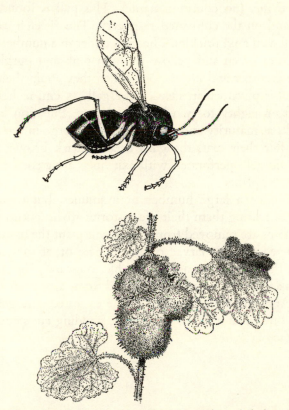

Fig. 23. *Liposthenus latreillei* (×9) with gall on Ground Ivy (Glechoma hederacea)

Xestophanes potentillae (no common name). Another gall-wasp parasitising a herbaceous plant, this species colonises the creeping cinquefoil (*Potentilla reptans*). The gall is fusiform (spindle-shaped) and affects the petiole or leaf-stalk; occasionally the eggs may be laid in the rhizome close to the surface of the soil.

The galls are pale green or pink at first, later turning brown. Usually a gall will contain six cells, each containing a larva. The cells are connected directly with the vascular channels of the plant through which nourishment is derived. The galls appear in July and mature in October, when the larvae pupate, overwintering in this stage, the imago emerging in the ensuing spring.

Diastrophus rubi (no common name). This gall is found both on bramble and on the cultivated raspberry. The affected stems swell and bear few, if any, prickles. The galls undergo a number of colour changes from green and yellow through pink and purple to light brown in October and November, when they attain their full size.

The gall is plurilocular, i.e., a large gall (15 cm. in length) may contain from eighty to two hundred larvae. Pupation takes place in the galls at maturity and the gall-wasps emerge in the following spring. After their exit, the galls become dark brown, hard and woody. Old galls perforated with exit holes are a common feature of established plants.

This gall has a large number of inquilines, but owing to the difficulty of rearing them their life-histories are little-known. When affected stems are removed from the parent plant the tissues become so contracted that the larvae cannot pupate or, if they succeed in doing so, the emerging imago is unable to escape. The best chance of success appears to be when the galled stems are cut in late March or early April immediately prior to the expected emergence of the adults and transplanted into damp soil; standing cut stems in water is unsatisfactory.

Appendices

How to Study Wasps

ONE advantage of choosing the Hymenoptera as a special subject of study is that this group of insects has very few devotees when compared with the more popular orders, such as butterflies and moths or the beetles. The immediate result of this is that there is a vast field for research, and even the beginner has a very good chance of discovering species new to his or her own country, or even new to science. Quite apart from this exciting possibility, the life-histories of a great number of wasps are unknown, and yet others are imperfectly known. Even the novice may unwittingly stumble upon new facts which fill the gaps in our knowledge, or start up a new line of enquiry.

One of the drawbacks to the study of the Hymenoptera is that there are so few books which do more than merely mention them in passing. Most of the literature of the group is spread throughout innumerable scientific journals, in which individual observers have recorded their findings in the form of papers; often these will be found in the annals of learned societies, spread over long periods of time, often extending over more than a hundred years. They certainly take some tracking down, but the effort is well worth while.

However, the most valuable contribution to our present knowledge which the beginner can make is not gained by reading the observations of his predecessors but by going out into the field and seeing for himself, making notes on the behaviour and other aspects of wasps in their natural habitat. If he has the opportunity to go abroad, he will discover for himself how different are the behaviour patterns and life-histories of wasps from different parts of the world, as we have already seen. The main point is to start out with an open mind and no preconceived notions of how the insects *ought* to behave in certain circumstances, because nature often decrees otherwise. When she does, she always has good reason for it; and one of the most fascinating tasks which face the student is to find out for himself what these reasons may be.

The equipment required for field study is not extensive, and the main items are a good pair of eyes and a field notebook. Keen observation and patience are the primary requirements, leaving no stone unturned, as the saying goes, or allowing any strange occurrence to go unqueried. Always make notes of your observations immediately, and do not trust to memory; no scientific value whatever can be attached to such statements as 'I think I saw so-and-so', or 'It might have been on such-and-such a day'. Not only must the observations themselves be fully described, but precise details must be given, preferably including the time of day (or night) as well as the date, and, of course, the locality.

This question of locality requires some consideration. It is useless to put, for example, 'taken near Guildford'; there is a Guildford in Dorset and a Guildford in Surrey. The county must be supplied, unless the locality is a county town like Hereford or Stafford. The word 'near' is too vague; 'seven miles north-west of Royston, Herts', is precise enough for all practical purposes, but if you want to be more scientific, it would be better still to use the Ordnance Survey Grid Map reference, taken from a one-inch or two-inch Ordnance Survey map. These maps are easy to read, and quoting the Grid reference numbers will leave the reader in no possible doubt as to the exact locality where your observations took place. If you are at any appreciable height above sea level, the altitude should also be stated.

Opinions differ as to the advisability of copying your original rough notes out into a more permanent record book. I personally certainly prefer to do this, as a neatly-typed loose-leaf ring-book is, to my way of thinking, a more legible record, as well as allowing space for far more than one's outdoor scribblings. Being larger, it also provides more scope for illustration by means of drawings, photographs, statistical tables, graphs and so on. However, I do see the point raised by many naturalists that one's original field notes, however rough they may be, should not be destroyed; they form a useful cross-reference to check with—provided one can read them!

The question of illustration can be interpreted very widely. The student who is gifted artistically can make his own sketches from life, either in pencil, drawing ink, or watercolour, which can be executed on separate sheets and inserted into the appropriate places in the book. Sketches may be fixed with clear varnish to avoid smudging, or the pages containing drawings can be interfaced with sheets of cellophane cut to the same size as the pages of the notebook.

If you are not handy with drawing materials, the camera can come to your rescue. Good photographs are quite easy to take, even with limited equipment. Either black-and-white or colour may be used, and even with a simple camera of the automatic type, plus a couple of meniscus lenses and filters, you should be able to come up with quite reasonable pictures. Of course, if you want to photograph very minute subjects, then you will need a camera with more potential, such as a twin-lens reflex type, complete with telephoto extension tubes. For the best results, you will also need electronic flash equipment.

Yet a third method of illustrating the field notebook is one very suited to the student of limited means: pictures can be cut out from magazines, newspapers and sometimes from publishers' advance book publicity material. Of course, this source will be somewhat limited, but even a few illustrations here and there will make your records more interesting. Old second-hand books, too, sometimes provide good pictures which could be used. Do not, however, be tempted to insert pictures which bear no relevance to the subject of your notes just because you have them available. The field notebook is not intended to be a scrapbook but a record of your own observations, supported by illustrations which have a direct bearing on your subject.

Instructions for making a reference collection are given in Appendix II. A small reference collection is really indispensable to the serious student; it does not need to be so large as to take up much space. One male, queen and worker of each species is normally sufficient, in the case of the social species, and one male and female of each of the solitary wasps. Carefully dried examples of wasps' nests may also be included in a collection, although these will, of course, take up more space.

There are enough different species of wasps in Britain alone to occupy the student's attention for many years of fascinating study, not to mention the thousands more species in other parts of the world. Wasps occur in almost every kind of habitat, and may be looked for in all weathers and at most times of the year. Hot sunny summer days will see most of the wasps on the wing, and late spring will be the peak season for the gall-wasps.

The absence of night-collecting, generally speaking, may make the collecting of Hymenoptera rather less exciting to an entomologist who has once sampled the joys of sugaring for moths or collecting at light; however, the odd wasp or two, including the hornet, does sometimes turn up at sugar along with slugs, hedgehogs and even less orthodox creatures. However, in the tropics the night-collector usually finds a larger proportion of wasps among his captures, as much to light as to sugar, ripe fruits and similar bait. It may be, of course, that there are so many more wasps around in the warmer regions, but a good number of them appear to be attracted to light and to sweet baits as a matter of course.

The young adventurer may find the element of risk in collecting wasps a challenge. There is at least some element of risk if you disturb a large community of wasps, but normally proper use of average common-sense will avoid this. In fact the wasp-collector is far less likely to be stung than the average bee-keeper, who rarely gets through a season without being stung.

The study of the sociality of the non-solitary species has no counterpart in any other branch of entomology. This aspect alone proves to be the most alluring angle of the study of Hymenoptera. The solitary species are scarcely less able to provide interesting examples of what the Reverend J. G. Wood was pleased to call 'homes without hands', some of which are unrivalled in ingenuity and beauty by any other members of the animal kingdom. In short, the Hymenoptera is the group for offering the student all he could possibly desire in variety, numbers of species and beauty, not to mention the fascination of their lives and habits, which are certainly more diverse than those of many other orders of insects. The actual collecting and field studies will take him into the fresh air and afford him plenty of exercise; he will not be able to observe, for example, the habits of the social wasps by poring over museum collections of dead specimens.

The identification of the smaller species—and even some of the bigger ones—may prove a stumbling-block to the beginner. It is very difficult to identify the Hymenoptera from books, especially the smaller ones; colour plates are not much help, because of the similarities in physical appearance between many members of the same genus, some of whose differences are so minute as to be hardly visible in a photograph. The keys which are normally used for identification purposes are very technical and difficult for a beginner to follow. The novice should attempt to familiarise himself first with the commoner members of the larger groups, making a small reference collection so that he can easily recognise them again in the field on future occasions. As he becomes more familiar with his material he will acquire a feeling for the group which will stand him in good stead as he gradually gets to know his way around the lesser-known, less familiar and smaller species. This is where a large museum collection can be very useful, and the curator of such a collection will usually prove extremely helpful to the serious student.

Another good idea is to join your local natural history society, whose members will be only too pleased to do their best to assist. You may well find that most of them are bird-watchers, botanists, lepidopterists or coleopterists, but as these persons usually spend a great deal of their spare time out of doors attending field meetings, many of them will be familiar with some of the Hymenoptera and very possibly able to identify at least some specimens for you, or, if they cannot, they will put you in touch with someone who can.

Unlike the butterfly and moth breeder, the hymenopterist will not find the breeding of wasps at all easy. Very little, comparatively speaking, has been achieved in this field. The gall-wasps can be bred out by collecting twigs bearing galled leaves. The twigs should be stood in moistened silver sand in tall glass containers; a piece of *very fine* muslin should be tied over the top of the container with a rubber band to prevent the escape of the emerging gall-wasps. Unfortunately you are just as likely to breed chalcids and other parasites out of the galls as the gall-wasps themselves, and until you get to know them, you will find this very confusing. Do not, however, be deterred; practically every year new ones are discovered, so this should encourage you to collect galls at every opportunity. They require no attention beyond the aforesaid insertion of the twigs into damp sand in securely-closed ventilated glass containers.

Keep different kinds of galls in separate containers; if you mix them up you will not know which insect has come from which gall. Most of these little creatures are extremely small, and if you want to study them you will need a microscope. This need not be a very high-powered model; a monocular type with magnifications ×25, ×50 and ×100 is perfectly adequate. The ability to draw clear sketches is very useful when studying these insects. Great works of art are not required; what is needed is a clear anatomical sketch showing the various parts of the body and, in particular, such minute details as the numbers of teeth in the antennae, the numbers of joints in the legs, and so on, as many of these characters are diagnostic. However, I am not going to pretend that it is easy, because some of the gall-wasps and their parasites—not to mention their hyperparasites and parasitoids—are less than 0·05 mm. in length.

Much easier is the study of solitary wasps, which can be attracted to your garden by the provision of artificial nesting-sites in the form of air-bricks placed on their sides against a sunny south-facing wall or fence (see Fig. 24). The holes in the bricks are colonised by various sphecids and other fossorial wasps such as *Oxybelus* and others, which are only too pleased to find a ready-made nesting-hole of exactly the right size.

To facilitate your own observations, ordinary glass test-tubes are inserted into the holes of the bricks. The figure shows the arrangement of the bricks to form an observation wall; these glass tubes will be colonised by female sphecid wasps who will build their cells along the entire length of the tubes and in which their broods can be seen in various stages of development.

Some observers have made these tubes out of lengths of elder

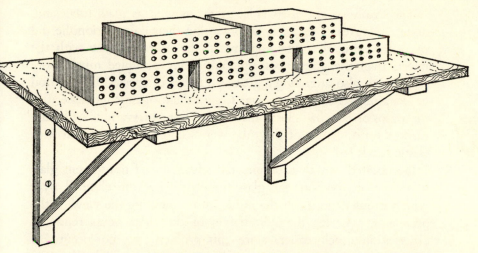

Fig. 24. Arrangement of bricks for insertion of glass tubes into air-holes. The supporting board should be firmly bracketed to a south-facing wall or fence.

stems, boring a hole through the pith, but since these stems are not transparent it is very difficult to do a great deal in the way of observing the activities within. One end, of course, is plugged with some impervious substance, and the female wasp can be seen going in and out, but I would not recommend this method when it is so much easier to have an unobstructed arena of observation by using glass tubes.

Each glass tube should be covered with a loose outer tube of brown paper, which can be easily removed by sliding the glass tube out of it. The tubes should be of such a diameter to allow them to fit easily into the holes in standard size air-bricks; these holes are in three rows of seven, eight, or nine, according to type. One of these bricks can therefore support twenty-one, twenty-four or twenty-seven observation tubes.

Professor Balfour-Browne, in his book *Concerning the Habits of Insects* (Cambridge University Press, 1925), described how he set up an observation wall using ten or more bricks, which were placed on their sides on a shelf in a sunny spot in his garden at Cambridge. He recorded that a great number of different species of wasps as well as bees used the facilities thus provided.

The Professor also used elder stems as well as glass tubes and, despite the greater difficulty in observing their colonisation, he did make the point that they appeared to be more popular with the insects than the glass tubes, not only being occupied much more rapidly but also attracting a greater number of species. His method of examining their contents was to split them open lengthwise after the wasps or bees had closed them, and after observations had been made the two halves of the tube were secured together again with elastic bands.

He pointed out that, despite the advantage of transparent glass tubes for observation, the glass frequently became clouded over with various deposits on the inside, thus obscuring the view of the occupants, whereas the split halves of the elder stems rendered observation much easier, since this problem did not occur. He also stated that a certain degree of humidity was essential, otherwise the contents of the tubes would dry out; but on the other hand, too moist a situation will encourage mould to form, and the larvae and pupae will die. It is essential, therefore, to maintain a reasonable balance between too dry or too wet a situation; a sunny spot should therefore have a certain amount of shelter and not be too exposed.

It was Balfour-Browne who devised a method of ascertaining the length of time the larvae lay in the cocoon before pupating, and how long the pupal stage lasted before the bee or wasp emerged. He cut a small window on the side of each cocoon, and by looking through this he was able to see the condition of the occupant.

The sub-terrarium

Earlier in this book I described the life-history of *Methoca ichneumonioides*, the wasp whose wingless females lay their eggs on the larvae of tiger beetles in their underground burrows. Hugh Main, writing in *The Essex Naturalist* in 1927 and again in 1931, described a method of rearing this species in such a way that they could be easily observed. These larvae spend nine months in the cocoon, and it is therefore essential to maintain their surroundings in a sufficiently damp condition to avoid desiccation, yet at the same time avoiding too wet conditions, which induce mould.

A straight-sided glass tumbler is used, with the lid of a glass-topped collecting-tin as a cover. Two oblong glass plates are cut, reaching to within an inch of the top. These plates are supported by about two inches of damp soil, and are supported vertically on one side by more soil, which should reach the top of the plates, but on the other side the soil should reach only about two inches up the side of the glass and level with the two inches or so of soil which lies between the two plates. On this a horizontal slip of glass is placed in order to prevent the tiger beetle larva from burrowing out of

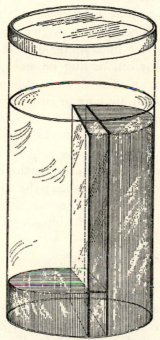

Fig. 25. Arrangement of sub-terrarium

sight. The space above this slip of glass is again filled with soil up to the level of the top of the plates. Figure 25 shows the arrangement diagramatically.

A shaft is made in the soil with a glass rod against one side of the tumbler (to be referred to as the 'front' of the tumbler for observation purposes), and a single tiger beetle larva is introduced. Hugh

Main described how he kept a number of such glasses, each containing a tiger beetle larva, and introduced a single *Methoca* female, transferring her from glass to glass as she laid her eggs, so that from the middle to the end of July in the following year eight adult wasps emerged from the nine eggs which had been laid (one per tiger beetle larva). Of these eight adults, three were females and five males; the ninth did not emerge.

From a series of such observations the life-cycle of *Methoca* can be followed with a minimum of care and attention and a maximum of observation potential.

With a sand-wasp such as *Ammophila*, one can follow a female bringing a caterpillar to her burrow. When she has carried it down and deposited an egg on it, filled up the shaft and, as it were, left the premises, the caterpillar can be dug up and transferred to a subterrarium for observation. For these sand-burrowing species it is easier to use a small aquarium tank or jar filled with sand, making a simulated burrow against the side of the tank with a glass rod. The caterpillar is then placed inside, and shielded from the light when no observations are being made by covering the outside of the tank with brown paper, which can be easily removed when required. It would seem to me very difficult to keep the adults of flying species such as *Ammophila* in captivity and provide them with the necessary food and conditions, but it is not too difficult to rear the subterranean larvae through their early stages.

Observations on the social vespids

If you find a wasps' nest which you can observe on the spot at regular intervals without much difficulty, it will be quite safe to do so, provided that you do not unduly disturb the community. However, if you have the opportunity of finding a thriving colony which is too far out of your way to render regular observations possible without too much trouble, it is quite a simple matter to transfer such a nest to your own garden or some other more convenient place, complete with wasps, without risking a single sting. If you are thinking of establishing a wasp community in your own garden, first, however, ensure that there will be no possibility of interference from, or danger to, children, or objections from parents or neighbours.

First of all you have to stupefy the wasps, but not kill them. This can be effected by squirting a few drops of chloroform into the entrance to the nest with a plastic syringe. Do not use too much, or you will destroy the whole community.

When all is quiet inside, you can saw off the part of the branch to which the nest is attached, if in a tree, or dig it up, if in the ground, and place the whole thing in a plastic bag. This should be closed to avoid the wasps escaping if they should happen to recover before you get the nest home. Be careful to avoid breathing the fumes.

The nest can be refastened to another branch with wire, or resited in a fresh hole in the ground, and the bag removed. A little fresh air will soon bring the wasps round again, and you can sit and watch them at a respectable distance and observe how they gradually get over the shock and start making orientation flights around the new site so as to familiarise themselves with it. Within a day or two at the most, the community will have settled down and resumed going about their daily business of foraging for food and feeding the grubs.

This brings me to a rather important point. The location in which you resite the nest must be one from which the wasps will be able to obtain their normal food supplies; in other words, it is of no use putting it in a garden which is assiduously cultivated, with the gardener spraying all the plants with insecticides, which will kill all the potential food-supply. Any survivors which remain will be so contaminated by the insecticides that the wasp grubs will be poisoned.

The ideal location for resiting a nest is in a small tract of woodland or farmland which is left more or less undisturbed. A 'wild' garden which has been allowed to become overgrown is also good; there will be plenty of caterpillars, flies, beetles and other insects among the weeds. The only hazard is going to be that in a good year a single queen may lay up to twenty-five thousand eggs, and the resultant plague of wasps may possibly be blamed on you!

If you want to obtain a complete wasps' nest containing dead wasps and brood *in situ* for study purposes, a safe way is to apply to your local council for the name and address of its pest exterminator, who will in most cases be pleased to assist. I have never yet been refused—unless he had no wasps' nests to offer! Pest exterminators in districts other than your own are equally co-operative, and you can, of course, apply to these in districts where *Vespula rufa, V. sylvestris* and other less common vespids occur, if they are not found in your own district. It should be pointed out that they deal only with the nest-building social wasps—they will not go out and spend the afternoon on their hands and knees hunting for *Eumenes coarctata* for you! I wish they would!

Making a Reference Collection

THE making of a reference collection of wasps is not exactly an easy pursuit. For one thing, it does not have the immediate attraction of the flamboyant colours of the butterflies and moths to recommend it. Unlike the lepidopterist, whose friends constantly ask him to bring out his drawers of specimens to show, not many people—except other hymenopterists—will ask him to bring out his drawers of wasps! On the other hand, the hymenopterist has far more chance than the lepidopterist of discovering new species; in fact new species are being discovered every year. If you keep your eyes open, it will be well within your scope to find a new wasp within your first three or four years of collecting, which may be not only new to your country but to science. This behoves you to keep a special lookout for the smaller or more obscure specimens, as these are the ones less likely to attract attention and, therefore, all the more likely to be overlooked.

The larger and brighter species are certainly known in the adult stage, but it is no exaggeration to say that a large proportion of them are either little-known, or even completely unknown, in their early stages. A really substantial contribution to our very incomplete knowledge of these can be made by even a beginner, frequently from some trivial observation which may be the vital link in a chain of unrelated facts, or it could be the first stepping-stone to the knowledge of a hitherto unknown life-history. This serves to emphasise the importance of keeping accurate records, as I pointed out in Appendix I.

The function of a reference collection is to enable the student to identify his or her specimens in the field. The basis of a good reference collection should, therefore, consist of at least one queen, one male and one worker of each of the social species, and a male and female of each of the solitary wasps.

The larger specimens can be set out much in the same way as butterflies and moths, but some of the very small species such as chalcids may prove too difficult to treat in this way, and are often better mounted in balsam as microscope slides. It is presumed that the student either possesses a microscope, or has access to one at a college or other educational establishment; one may sometimes be borrowed from a natural history society of which the student is a member.

A very powerful instrument is not required; a simple monocular microscope with a magnification of up to × 100 is perfectly adequate. However, I am not going into detail about making microscope slide mounts, as this is dealt with in the many excellent books on the subject (see Appendix IV).

For collecting in the field, the same kind of equipment as that used by the lepidopterist is usually sufficient; this comprises a net, killing bottle and glass-bottomed boxes for transporting live specimens as well as flat tins or boxes for the dead ones. Glass tubes are better than boxes for the small species. The net need not be so big as that used by the lepidopterist.

The killing agent used is a matter of choice; I have always found chloroform to be the most satisfactory, and it is also the least dangerous of the various poisons. For wasps, the killing bottle need not be very big, but a plastic bottle should not be used, as some chemicals—chloroform included—distort plastic and cloud it. Some large plastic bags in which to collect and transport wasps' nests (see Appendix I) are very useful. Don't forget the wire closures!

The same procedures as those adopted by the lepidopterist will be successful in netting Hymenoptera which have settled on flowers, etc. Beating and sweeping may also be employed. The vegetation at the bottom of hedgerows, especially if overgrown with various weeds, will frequently produce an interesting assortment of species; the same applies to beating the lower branches of trees and bushes, especially when these are in bloom. The biggest catches, however, will usually be from flower-heads in sunny meadows and similar situations on warm days.

Wasps, being lovers of sunlight, are less in evidence in shady woodlands, but it is always worth while to try them also, in the hope of securing species which may be less easily obtained elsewhere. One of the best types of habitat to explore systematically is a sandy locality such as a gravel-pit or coastal sand-dunes; nearly all the sand-wasps such as *Ammophila* are found in such habitats.

Heaths and commons, especially those on sandy soil, are very good wasp localities, and a large proportion of the solitary species can be found there, including *Eumenes coarctata*.

Difficulty may be experienced when collecting the smaller species. The gall-wasps are easy enough to breed out if you collect the twigs bearing the galls and stand them upright in tall glass or plastic containers with their ends in damp silver sand. The open top of the container must be firmly secured by a piece of very fine-meshed material held in place with a rubber band. It is important to avoid mixing up the different kinds of gall in one container, as you would not know which wasps had emerged from which galls.

This particular group is one which has great potential for new discoveries, so it is very important to avoid unwittingly causing confusion by making mistakes in identification. Chalcids, braconids and the hyperparasites of both will certainly emerge as well as the gall-wasps themselves, and sorting out which is which will be a fascinating puzzle. As a rule the primary parasite will be a little smaller than the gall-wasp, and the hyperparasite will be considerably smaller than either. A microscope is essential for anyone who intends to study these groups.

The preservation of the larger species is carried out in a similar fashion to that of butterflies and moths. Small setting-boards are used; these need not necessarily be the standard 14 inch length used for butterflies and moths; since wasps are, on the whole, smaller than many Lepidoptera, many more can be set on one board, and if the board is very long and you have a large number to set, it may be awkward to manage. However, this is a matter of personal choice.

Setting Hymenoptera

The method of setting is the same as that used for Lepidoptera, with the exception that the entomological pin used is not put through

145

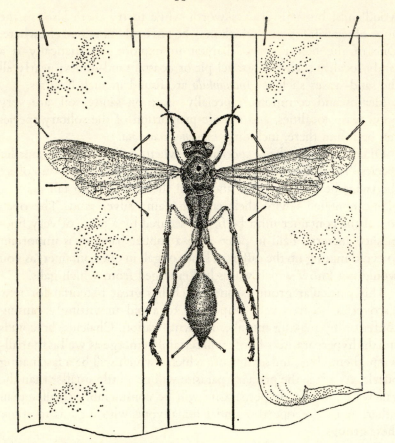

Fig. 26. Method of setting wasps. The species shown is *Mischocyttarus melanarius* from South America, twice natural size.

the centre of the thorax but slightly to the right of the median line; this is standard museum practice. The difficulty is that when the body is very thin it is difficult to get the pin through it at all. A good hand lens is useful in these cases.

Tracing-paper or transparent cellophane is cut into strips slightly narrower than the width of the sides of the board, and secured at the top edge by two glass-headed pins (or their plastic equivalent if glass-headed ones are unobtainable). The method is to spread the wings as shown in Figure 26; the main point is to avoid puncturing the wing with the setting-pins, which may be of the ordinary domestic or office kind, as entomological pins are too thin to be used for this purpose. The paper strips are secured around the edges of the wings, and the body may be supported by one or two pins if necessary. The antennae should be set out symmetrically, as also the legs. A small space should be left between each specimen on the board so as to avoid the appendages of one specimen knocking against those of the next and damaging them.

Labelling

The data label is very important; without this the specimen is valueless from the scientific point of view. If you do a lot of collecting in one locality, you can have labels printed in small type with the locality as well as your name, leaving a dotted line between them for the date of capture. If you collect in various localities, you can either have labels printed with your name, leaving two lines for the date and the locality, or you can write out your labels by hand if you can write small enough.

These labels, which go on the pins under the specimens, are normally much smaller than those used for butterflies and moths, and as a rule it is better to have them printed in tiny type. They look much neater and much more uniform, and it is almost impossible to write as small as one would wish. Nothing looks worse than big labels sticking out below small specimens; such oversize labels can also damage the legs of the specimens, or knock off the bodies when handled.

Do not be tempted to use only numbers on the labels, referring to a card index catalogue or some such system. It may *look* very good, but you have only to lose the catalogue, and your entire collection has had its lot. You yourself may not lose the catalogue, but one must also consider posterity, when the collection may pass into other hands, and in the absence of the catalogue its value would be lost.

Preservation of specimens

Wasps take much less time to dry out than butterflies and moths; a few days is usually sufficient, even for the larger species. After carefully removing them from the boards, they can be housed either in double-sided storeboxes or a cabinet, in the same way as butterflies and moths. Mites, museum beetles and other pests can be avoided by the use of either naphthalene or paradichlorbenzene, which should be renewed regularly, If cells for this purpose are not provided in the drawer or box, one can be made by cutting out a triangle of cardboard and supporting it on two oblongs of the same material glued to one of the front corners of the box or drawer. The cardboard should be pierced with small holes before filling with the crystals the cell thus formed and covering the top with the triangular piece, which is then glued in place.

Another method used in museum collections is to put the crystals in a small glass tube, which is stoppered with a plug of cottonwool and secured with cellotape to the bottom of the box or drawer in as inconspicuous a place as possible. This method has the advantage that the evaporation of the crystals can be seen at a glance through the glass tube, and renewed as required.

Grease and mould, which frequently attack collections of Lepidoptera, seldom wreak havoc with wasp collections, because their bodies are so much thinner and do not contain the quantities of fatty matter more in evidence in the thicker-bodied moths. The possible exception to this is with certain very large tropical wasps, but if these are properly dried out immediately after capture, even these are unlikely to be affected. The undersides of the bodies may be painted with mercuric chloride (corrosive sublimate) if desired. (**NOTE:** *This substance is a deadly poison and must be kept well out of the reach of children and unauthorised persons.*) In damp climates, a few crystals of silica gel in a muslin bag affixed to one corner of the container will have the effect of absorbing any moisture.

Wasps should be arranged in systematic order, with the names of the groups and families at the top of the columns and the generic and specific names at the bottom. Some collectors prefer to put the generic names at the top also, with only the specific names below the specimens. Appendix III consists of a label list of all the British Hymenoptera-Aculeata (excluding bees and ants) which should be found useful, being printed on one side only so that it may be detached and cut up for use.

These labels are usually fixed to the box or drawer with headless stainless steel labelling points. Since these latter are now difficult to obtain, a satisfactory substitute can be made by cutting off the point ends of ordinary entomological pins to a length of about $\frac{3}{8}$ inch with wire-cutters.

Carding and pointing

We come now to the preservation of the smaller species such as chalcids or gall-wasps. If you wish to make microscope slides, all well and good, but this has the disadvantage that the specimens cannot be examined from all angles unless you mount several specimens in different positions. In the usual method of 'carding' and 'pointing' the specimens are set in the normal way, using a dissecting-lens to facilitate this operation, and then gummed on tiny triangular pieces of paper known as 'points'. The gum used must be transparent. One such gum is gum arabic; another is gum tragacanth. Each has its devotees, and some use a mixture of the two; there is not much to choose between them—except the price. Only the tiniest drop of gum should be used—as much as can be suspended from a pin-point without dropping off—just sufficient to secure the point of the card triangle to the side of the specimen. The latter should overhang the card so that the legs, wings, etc. on one side are free of gum. This method has the disadvantage that the specimens cannot be easily viewed under the microscope, although of course a good lens can be used. An entomological pin is then thrust through the wide end of the card, and the label attached below this.

Some workers turn up the extreme tip of the point and glue this to the side of the specimen; but this is not only difficult to do, but frequently causes breakage to the specimen, and is not recommended. The points also have an irritating habit of 'unbending', with the result that the specimen usually snaps off the point.

Preservation in tubes of spirit is not normally used for Hymenoptera, except for grubs or pupae if these are required to be preserved for microscopic examination or other purposes.

Staging

Specimens which are too large for carding and pointing but are rather too small for ordinary pinning can be staged. This method involves pinning them through the thorax with very fine stainless steel headless pins; the specimens are then set, and after removal from the board the headless point is thrust into a strip of polyporus pith. Several specimens can be staged on one strip of pith if preferred, but these should be all of one species. The pith, or 'stage', is then pinned through the opposite end with an ordinary entomo-

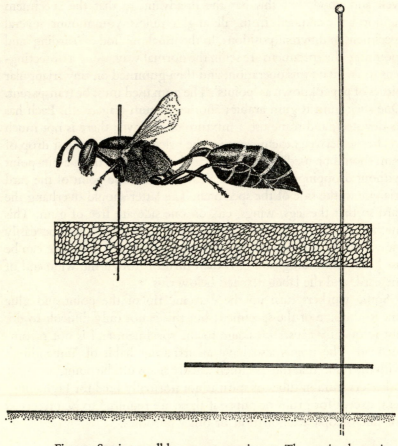

Fig. 27. Staging small hymenopterous insects. The species shown is
Polybia platycephala (×6)

logical pin (see Fig. 27), and inserted into the cork of a storebox or cabinet drawer in the usual way.

Identification

The foregoing should be sufficient to enable the student to form a good reference collection of Hymenoptera, but the most difficult part will be not the mechanics of making the collection but the correct identification of species, which is of course the primary object of making such a collection. Only a great deal of practice and practical field experience will enable the collector to identify his specimens with any degree of certainty. By the end of his first year he should be able to recognise the commoner species, and to recognise the main groups and families, even if he is not always able to differentiate between the genera or species. This, too, will become easier with practice, but it must be strongly emphasised that as much help as possible be sought from those who are more familiar with the Hymenoptera as a whole, and that no opportunity should be lost of comparing specimens with those in museums and other large collections.

This book does not set out to be a reference book for the identification of species; all it can do is to encourage the student to learn about the habits of wasps, to know where to look for them, and to endeavour to understand their behaviour. It would be quite impossible in a work of this size to attempt to describe all known species, even only of all the wasps found in Britain.

The process of learning, through difficult identifications and the use of elaborate keys, is a long and challenging one, but it brings one into contact with those who have already familiarised themselves with the Hymenoptera as a group, and these persons are only too ready to help the beginner. Added to this is the personal knowledge gained from active field collecting and observation, which take the student into many different kinds of habitat, and the more he does this the easier his task will become. There is also always the possibility that he may make some exciting discovery. If the student enjoys this task even one-tenth as much as I have done, then I shall be amply rewarded.

Label List of British Social and Solitary Wasps

This list is printed on one side of the page only so that it may be detached and cut up for labelling specimens in a reference collection, as described in Appendix II.

BRITISH SOCIAL WASPS

Family VESPIDAE

Vespa crabro (L.)

Vespula vulgaris (L.)

Vespula germanica (Fab.)

Vespula rufa (L.)

Vespula austriaca (Panz.)

Vespula sylvestris (Scop.)

Vespula norvegica (Fab.)

BRITISH SOLITARY WASPS

Family VESPIDAE

Pseudepipona quadrifasciata (Fab.)

Pseudepipona herrichii Sauss.

Ancistrocerus callosus (Thom.)

Ancistrocerus parietum (L.)

Ancistrocerus pictus (L.)

Ancistrocerus trimarginatus (Zett.)

Ancistrocerus albotricinctus (Zett.)

Ancistrocerus antilope (Panz.)

Symmorphus crassicornis (Panz.)

Symmorphus elegans (Westm.)

Symmorphus sinuatissimus Richards

Symmorphus bifasciatus (L.)

Family *EUMENIDAE*

Eumenes coarctata (L.)

Odynerus spinipes (L.)

Odynerus melanocephalus (Gm.)

Odynerus reniformis (Gm.)

Odynerus laevipes (Sh.)

Microdynerus exilis (H–S.)

Family *CLEPTIDAE*

Cleptes semiaurata (L.)

Cleptes nitidula (Fab.)

Family *CHRYSIDIDAE*

Notosus constrictus Forster

Ommalus truncatus (Dahlbohm)

Ommalus aeneus (Fab.)

Ommalus auratus (L.)

Ommalus violaceus (Scop.)

Holopyga gloriosa (Fab.)

Hedychrum nobile (Scop.)

Hedychrum intermedium Dahlbohm

Hedychridium roseum (Rossi)
Hedychridium integrum (Dahlbohm)
Hedychridium coriaceum (Dahlbohm)
Hedychridium ardens (Latreille)
Spintharis neglecta (Sh.)
Chrysis pustulosa (Ab.)
Chrysis hirsuta (Gerst.)
Chrysis cyanea (L.)
Chrysis ignita (L.)
Chrysis ruddii (Sh.)
Chrysis succincta L.
Chrysis viridula L.

Family TIPHIDAE

Tiphia femorata (Fab.)
Tiphia minuta (van den L.)

Family SAPYGIDAE

Sapyga quinquepunctata (Fab.)
Sapyga clavicornis (L.)

Family METHOCIDAE

Methoca ichneumonioides Latreille

Family MYRMOSIDAE

Myrmosa melanocephala (Panz.)

Family MUTILLIDAE

Mutilla europaea (L.)
Mutilla (Smicromyrme) rufipes (Fab.)

Family *POMPILIDAE*

Cryptocheilus affinis (van den L.)

Priocnemis perturbator (Harris)

Priocnemis coriaceus Dahlbohm

Priocnemis clementi Haupt.

Priocnemis minor (Zett.)

Priocnemis exaltatus (Fab.)

Priocnemis femoralis Dahlbohm

Priocnemis obtusiventris Schiödte

Priocnemis cordivalvatus Haupt.

Priocnemis pusillus Schiödte

Priocnemis gracilis Haupt.

Priocnemis schiödtei Haupt.

Priocnemis propinquus (Lep.)

Calicurgus hyalinatus (Fab.)

Deuteragenia hircana (Fab.)

Deuteragenia variegata (L.)

Deuteragenia intermedia Dahlbohm

Pseudagenia carbonaria (Scop.)

Pompilus plumbeus (Fab.)

Pompilus sericeus (van den L.)

Pompilus minutulus Dahlbohm

Pompilus spissus Schiödte

Pompilus unguicularis Thom.

Pompilus trivialis Dahlbohm

Pompilus westmaeli Thom.

Pompilus consobrinus Dahlbohm

Pompilus rufus Haupt.

Pompilus crassicornis Sh.

Evagetes dubius (van den L.)

Anoplius fuscus (L.)
Anoplius infuscatus (van den L.)
Anoplius nigerrimus (Scop.)
Anoplius concinnus (Dahlbohm)
Anoplius piliventris (Mor.)
Episyron rufipes (L.)
Aporus unicolor Spin.
Homonotus sanguinolentus (Fab.)
Ceropales variegata (Fab.)
Ceropales maculata (Fab.)

Family *SPHECIDAE*

Astata boops (Schr.)
Astata stigma (Klug.)
Tachysphex nitidus (Spin.)
Tachysphex pompiliformis (Panz.)
Tachysphex lativalvis (Thom.)
Dynetus pictus (Fab.)
Miscophus concolor Dahlbohm
Miscophus maritimus Smith
Trypoxylon figulus (L.)
Trypoxylon clavicerum Lep.
Trypoxylon attenuatum Smith
Ammophila sabulosa (L.)
Ammophila campestris Latreill
Podalonia viatica (L.)
Podalonia affinis (Kirby)
Spilomena troglodytes (van den L.)
Stigmus solskyi (Mor.)
Pemphredon lugubris (Fab.)

Cemonus shuckardi Mor.

Cemonus rugifer Dahlbohm

Cemonus westmaeli Mor.

Cemonus scoticus (Perkins)

Cemonus lethifer Sh.

Ceratophorus morio (van den L.)

Ceratophorus clypealis (Thom.)

Diodontus minutus (Fab.)

Diodontus insidiosus Spooner

Diodontus luperus Sh.

Passaloecus corniger Sh.

Passaloecus insignis (van den L.)

Passaloecus gracilis (Curt.)

Passaloecus monilicornis Dahlbohm

Mimesa shuckardi Westm.

Mimesa equestris (Fab.)

Mimesa rufa (Panz.)

Mimesa unicolor (van den L.)

Mimesa dahlbohmi Westm.

Psen ater (Fab.)

Psenulus atratus (Fab.)

Psenulus concolor (Dahlbohm)

Oxybelus uniglumis (L.)

Oxybelus sericeatus Gerst.

Oxybelus argentatus Curt.

Crabro cribrarius (L.)

Crabro scutellatus (Sch.)

Crabro peltarius (Schreb.)

Crabro leucostomoides Richards

Crabro pubescens (Sh.)

Crabro cetratus (Sh.)

Crabro capitosus (Sh.)

Crabro styrius (Kohl)

Crabro ambiguus (Dahlbohm)

Crabro walkeri (Sh.)

Crabro leucostomus (L.)

Acanthocrabro vagabundus (Panz.)

Hoplocrabro quadrimaculatus (Fab.)

Hoplocrabro clypeatus (Schreb.)

Metacrabro lituratus (Panz.)

Metacrabro quadricinctus (Fab.)

Blepharipus dimidiatus (Fab.)

Ablepharipus podagricus (van den L.)

Crossocerus tarsatus (Sh.)

Crossocerus palmipes (L.)

Crossocerus varus (L. and B.)

Crossocerus anxius (Westm.)

Crossocerus westmaeli (van den L.)

Crossocerus elongatus (van den L.)

Crossocerus exiguus (van den L.)

Clytochrysus zonatus (Panz.)

Clytochrysus planifrons (Thom.)

Clytochrysus cavifrons (Thom.)

Clytochrysus chrysostomus (L. and B.)

Solenius rubicola (D. and P.)

Solenius continuus (Fab.)

Ectemnibus dives (L. and B.)

Corynopus coarctatus (Scop.)

Corynopus nigrinus (Kies.)

Rhopalum clavipes (L.)

Lindenius panzeri (van den L.)

Lindenius albilabris (Fab.)

Lindenius armatus (Fab.)

Entomognathus brevis (van den L.)

Nysson spinosus (Forster)

Nysson interruptus (Fab.)

Nysson trimaculatus (Rossi)

Nysson dimidiatus Jur.

Gorytes mystaceus (L.)

Gorytes fargei Sh.

Hoplisus quadrifasciatus (Fab.)

Hoplisus laticinctus (Lep.)

Hoplisus bicinctus (Rossi)

Harpactus tumidus (Panz.)

Didyneus lunicornis (Fab.)

Mellinus arvensis (L.)

Mellinus sabulosus (Fab.)

Philanthus triangulum (Fab.)

Cerceris ribensis (L.)

Cerceris sabulosa (Panz.)

Cerceris quadricincta (Panz.)

Cerceris arenaria (L.)

Cerceris quinquefasciata (Rossi)

Cerceris cunicularia (Schr.)

Books for Further Reading

Amateur Entomologists' Society	Hymenopterist's Handbook	A.E.S., 1969
Andrewes, Sir Christopher	The Lives of Wasps and Bees	Chatto and Windus, 1969
Beeler, N. F. and Branley, F. M.	Experiments with a Microscope	Faber, 1958
Crompton, John	The Hunting Wasp	Collins, 1948
Evans, H. E.	Wasp Farm	Harrap, 1964
Evans, H. E. and Eberhard, M. J. W.	The Wasps	University of Michigan Press, 1970
Fabre, J. H.	The Hunting Wasps	Hodder and Stoughton, 1915
Imms, A. D.	Insect Natural History	Collins, 1947
Imms, A. D.	Social Behaviour in Insects	Methuen, 1931
Peckham, G. W. and Peckham, E. G.	Wasps, Social and Solitary	Constable, 1905
Richards, O. W.	The Social Insects	Macdonald, 1953

Step, Edward	Bees, Wasps, Ants and Allied Insects of the British Isles	Warne, 1932
Wheeler, W. M.	Social Life among the Insects	Constable, 1923

Glossary

Abdomen: the third division of the insect body

Abdominal: pertaining to the abdomen

Aculeata: the division of the Hymenoptera comprising the wasps, bees and ants

Aculeate: lit. 'needle-pointed', i.e., furnished with a sting

Air-brick: a brick perforated with numerous air-holes used for ventilating buildings

Alternating generations: two generations produced within a single life-cycle, one producing individuals of one sex only and the other producing both sexes

Antennae: in insects, paired sensory organs on the head

Apical: pertaining to the apex, or highest point

Aphids: plant-lice, greenfly, blackfly

Apocrita: the division of the Hymenoptera comprising the Aculeata and the Parasitica

Aquatic: living in the water

Arboreal: living in trees

Assassin-bug: a member of the family Reduviidae of the order Hemiptera

Auxiliary burrow: an additional burrow made by a wasp but not used as the main burrow for the nest

Barbed: furnished with barbs or teeth, as a bee's sting

Basal: pertaining to the base, or lowest point

Bedeguar: the moss-gall, ragged robin or robin's pincushion

Bee-fly: a member of the family Bombylidae of the order Diptera

Beeswax: wax secreted by the wax glands of the bee

Bignell tray: a tray used by entomologists for beating insects from bushes, etc.

Bisexual generation: the second of two alternating generations (q.v.) producing individuals of both sexes

Braconid: a small parasitic wasp of the family Braconidae

Brassica: a member of the cabbage family of plants

Brood: the eggs, larvae and pupae of wasps and bees

Brood-cell: a cell containing a wasp or bee egg, larva or pupa in the nest

Brood-chamber: a larger type of cell containing several individuals in their early stages

Bug: in the strict sense an insect which is a member of the order Hemiptera

Bumble-bee: another name for the humble-bee

Caddis-case: the case made by the caddis-worm (q.v.) for protection, in which it lives

Caddis-fly: an adult insect of the order Trichoptera

Caddis-worm: the larva of a caddis-fly (q.v.)

Cambium: the layer in the plant body through which nutrient materials are drawn up from the roots

Camouflage: the resemblance of an animal to its surroundings for protection against its enemies

Canopy: the envelope or outer paper covering of the nest of certain social wasps

Carnivorous: meat-eating

Carton: a tough cardboard-like material made by certain wasps for their nest-covering

Cell: a division, usually hexagonal, in which an egg is laid by the queen wasp or bee in the nest

Cercopid: a frog-hopper or plant-bug of the family Cercopidae

Chafer: a beetle of the family Melolonthidae

Chalcid: a small parasitic wasp of the superfamily Chalcidoidea

Cicada: a stridulating insect of the order Orthoptera found in tropical and sub-tropical regions

Clearwings: moths of the family Sesiidae

Cocoon: the silken outer covering containing the pupal stage of an insect

Coleoptera: the order of Beetles

Coleopterist: a person who studies beetles
Coleopterous: pertaining to the Coleoptera
Colonial: living in close proximity, but not necessarily in any social organisation
Colony: a group of individuals living close together, but not necessarily socially-orientated
Column: the central pillar supporting a wasps' nest
Columnar: pertaining to a column
Comb: the supporting structure built at right angles to the central nest support which contains the cells
Commensal: an animal living with another animal species which neither harms nor confers benefit upon it
Commensalism: the living together of two animal species in a mutual relationship which is neither harmful nor beneficial one to another
Community: a socially-orientated group of animals of one species
Compound eyes: eyes consisting of many facets, as opposed to simple eyes
Concave: curved inwards
Concavity: an inwardly-curved surface or depression
Construction gland: a gland producing a size-like substance in wasps to enable them to make paper from wood-pulp
Convex: curved outwards
Convexity: an outwardly-curved surface or excrescence
Corrosive sublimate: another name for mercuric chloride
Cross-pollination: a mechanism to ensure pollination of different individual plants and to avoid self-pollination
Cross-section: a cutting across the widest part of a structure to show the internal form
Cuckoo species: an animal species which deposits its egg or young in the nest of another species, leaving the latter parent to rear it, like the cuckoo
Cuckoo-spit: the frothy substance produced by the frog-hopper or cercopid (q.v.)
Cynipid: a member of the gall-wasps or Cynipoidea

Diagnostic character: a physical characteristic which may help to distinguish one species from another

173

Diapause: a resting stage in insects during which metabolism is lowered and the insects are dormant

Diptera: the order of two-winged flies

Dipterist: a person who studies the Diptera

Dipterous: pertaining to the Diptera

Discoid: disc-shaped

Distal: the end of an appendage furthest from its juncture with the body

Domesticated: used by man to provide him with its products, as the honey-bee

Dorsal: the upper surface of the body

Driver ants: tropical ants living in vast colonies

Drone: a male wasp or bee

Drone-fly: a member of the family Syrphidae of the order Diptera

Dry season: the period between monsoons when no rain falls, in certain tropical regions

Dung-beetle: a member of various groups of beetles which lay their eggs in dung

Ecology: the study of the relationships of plants and animals to their environment and to each other

Egg-cocoon: a silken sac containing eggs laid by certain spiders

Entomologist: a person who studies insects

Entomology: the study of insects

Environment: surroundings

Enzyme: a substance secreted in the body to assist digestion

Excrescence: a protuberance

Excretion: the function of expelling waste materials from the body

False burrow: a burrow intended to mislead predators, which is not used for nesting

Fanning: the vibration of the wings of wasps or bees to reduce nest-temperature

Fertilisation: the impregnation of the female by the male

Filament: a thread-like process

Filamentous: thread-like

Foliated: covered with leaves

Foraging: searching for and collecting food

Fossorial: digging in earth or sand

Foundation-pillar: the central support of a nest

Frog-hopper: a plant-bug of the family Cercopidae of the order Hemiptera

Fusiform: spindle-shaped

Gall: a swelling on a part of a plant caused by the activities of an insect or, more rarely, a fungus or other organism

Gall-causer: the organism which causes a gall to form

Gall-midge: a member of the family Cecidomyidae of the order Diptera

Gall-wasp: a member of the superfamily Cynipoidea of the order Hymenoptera-Parasitica

Genus: a group of closely related species within a family

Geometer: a larva of a group of moths characterised by the 'looping' movement of their caterpillars; an adult moth of this group

Geometrid: pertaining to the Geometers

Globular: globe-shaped

Grub: an insect larva

Habitat: the kind of environment in which a plant or animal normally lives

Habitat-specific: adapted to live only in one particular kind of habitat

Hibernaculum: a place chosen for hibernation

Hibernation: the winter sleep

Hindgut: the posterior part of the alimentary canal

Hive bee: the honey-bee

Honey: the sweet substance produced by the honey-bee

Honey-bee: the hive bee

Horizontal: at right angles to the vertical

Hormone: a substance secreted by glands into the bloodstream

Hornet: a large vespid wasp

Horntail: the wood-wasp

Host: the animal on which another animal species is parasitic

Host-specific: adapted only in relation to parasitism of one particular species

Hover-fly: a member of the family Syrphidae of the order Diptera

Humble-bee: a bumble-bee

Hymenoptera: the order to which wasps, bees and ants belong

Hymenopterist: a person who studies Hymenoptera

Hymenopterous: pertaining to the Hymenoptera

Hyper-parasite: the parasite of a parasite

Hypothesis: an informed conjecture based on probabilities

Ichneumon: a member of the family Ichneumonidae of the order Hymenoptera-Parasitica

Imago (pl. imagines): the perfect state of an insect; the adult stage

Inquiline: a species of insect inhabiting a gall which is not the primary gall-causer, not necessarily parasitic upon the gall-causer

Insecticide: a toxic chemical substance used to destroy insects by gardeners

Integument: the outer covering of the insect body

Isoptera: the order of Termites

Katydid: a kind of longhorned grasshopper native to America

Larva (pl. larvae): the second stage in the life-cycle of an insect which undergoes complete metamorphosis

Larval: pertaining to the larva

Leaf-cutter bee: a bee of the family Megachilidae which cuts circular or oval pieces out of leaves or petals to line its nest

Leaf-hopper: a kind of plant-bug of the order Hemiptera

Lepidoptera: the Butterflies and Moths

Lepidopterist: a person who studies butterflies and moths

Lepidopterous: pertaining to the Lepidoptera

Life-cycle: the complete series of stages through which an insect passes from the egg to maturity

Ligneous: woody

Lignivorous: wood-eating

Littoral: living on the seashore

Looper: the larva of a Geometrid moth (q.v.)

Mandibles: jaws or biting mouthparts

Marginal: pertaining to the margin

Marram-grass: the coarse grass which grows on sand-dunes

Mass-provisioning: provisioning the nest or cell with all the food required by the larva to last it until pupation at once, and then sealing the cell or nest

Masticate: to chew

Matriarchal community: a community dominated by the queen; an all-female society, commonly found in the social insects

Membranous: membrane-like

Mercuric chloride: corrosive sublimate

Mitotic division: simple division into two cells by a single cell, causing growth of the organism

Monsoon: a period of heavy rains which occurs in certain tropical regions

Multi-layered: composed of many layers or tiers

Museum beetle: a beetle of the genus *Anthrenus* which consumes dried museum specimens

Mutillid: a wasp of the family Mutillidae, known popularly as 'velvet ants' owing to the ant-like appearance of the wingless females

Nectar: a sweet substance produced by flowers to attract wasps, bees and other insects and thus ensure pollination

Nitrogenous wastes: waste products of the body containing nitrogen and other materials

Noctuid: a moth of the superfamily Noctuae

Nomenclature: the naming of plant and animal species, genera, families, orders, etc.

Nuptial flight: the mating flight of the queen wasp, bee or ant

Nymph: the second stage in the life-cycle of an insect which undergoes incomplete metamorphosis

Ocelli: simple eyes without facets

Overwintering: passing the winter in any stage of development

Oviposit: to lay eggs

Oviposition: egg-laying

Ovipositor: egg-placing organ in female insects
Ovo-viviparous: laying eggs which immediately hatch into larvae
Ovum (pl. ova): an egg

Pabulum: material used as food
Palps: sensory organs of insects situated on the head
Parasite: an animal which lives at the expense of another species
Parasitic: the habit of a parasite
Parasitica: the group of the Hymenoptera comprising the ichneumons, chalcids and gall-wasps
Parasitise: to live as a parasite in or upon another animal species
Parasitoid: the parasite of a hyper-parasite (q.v.)
Parthogenetic: being able to reproduce without fertilisation by the male
Pedicel: the central supporting pillar of a wasps' nest on which the combs are arranged at right angles
Petiole: the slender 'wasp-waist' in wasps, actually the attenuated first abdominal segment
Pentatomid bug: a member of the family Pentatomidae or shield-bugs of the order Hemiptera
Physiological: pertaining to the body structure
Phytophagous: plant-eating
Pillar: the central column supporting a wasps' nest
Pith: the woody material in plant stems
Plant-lice: aphids, greenfly, blackfly
Poikilothermic: having a body temperature the same as that of the surroundings; popularly called 'cold-blooded'
Pollen: the fertilising agent produced by the male stamens in the flowering plants
Polyporus: a bracket-fungus which grows on trees
Primary gall-causer: the insect or other organism which originally causes the appearance of a gall on a plant
Predaceous: preying upon other animals
Predator: an animal which preys upon other animals
Predatory: of predaceous habits
Progressive provisioning: the feeding of the grub with food as and when required until it is fully-fed

Propodeum: a thoracic excrescence in certain Hymenoptera

Protective coloration: the external coloration of an animal to enable it to blend into its surroundings, thus affording protection from its enemies

Protective resemblance: a resemblance of an animal to its background to afford protection from predators

Protein: the vital nutritive substance necessary for growth

Provisioning: feeding the young by stocking the nest

Proximal: the end of an appendage nearest to its juncture with the body

Pubescence: a covering of soft downy hairs

Pupa (pl. pupae): the third stage in the life-cycle of an insect which undergoes complete metamorphosis

Pupal: appertaining to the pupa

Pupation: the act of changing from the larva into the pupa or resting-stage in insects which undergo a complete metamorphosis

Queen: the foundress of a colony; the matriarchal head of a wasp or bee community; an egg-laying female wasp or bee. The term is also used with the ants

Ragged robin: the rose bedeguar gall

Reconnaissance flight: the first flight of a newly-emerged wasp or bee to learn the position of the nest or hive

Regurgitation: the expulsion of partly-processed food from the crop to feed the young grubs by the workers

Rhizome: a root

Robin's pincushion: the rose bedeguar gall

Saliva: a fluid produced from glands in the mouthparts

Sawfly: a member of the Symphyta, a sub-division of the order Hymenoptera

Scavenger: an animal which feeds upon the detritus left by other organisms

Segment: a part of the body between the chitinous rings of the abdomen; a part of an appendage between the joints, especially of antennae

Setting: the art of spreading the wings, antennae and legs of a preserved insect so as to show the various parts clearly

Setting-board: a board made of wood and cork to enable setting to be carried out

Shaft: the part of an underground burrow between the entrance-hole and the nest-chamber

Shield-bug: a member of the family Pentatomidae of the order Hemiptera

Silica gel: a crystalline chemical substance which is strongly water-absorbent, used in extracting moisture from preserved collections, especially in moist conditions and humid climates

Simple eyes: the ocelli, or eyes without facets

Social: living together and working together for the common good in a community

Sociality: the state of living as a social unit

Solitary: the opposite of the social habit; living as a single unit

Species: one type of named animal or plant, as distinct from another

Species dispersal: the mechanism of ensuring that a species becomes more widely distributed so as to encourage survival of the species and to avoid too much competition for food and territory in a limited area

Specialisation: in predatory insects, the habit of keeping only to one type or species of prey animal as food

Spherical: shaped like a sphere

Spinnerets: the silk-producing glands of spiders at the rear end of the body

Stage: a strip of polyporus pith used in mounting small insect specimens

Staging: the art of mounting small specimens on polyporus pith

Sterile: incapable of reproduction

Sterile female: in wasps and bees which live in social communities, a non-reproductive worker

Stimulus: an occurrence which triggers off a reaction

Sting: a tube attached to a poison-sac, with a needle-sharp end for injecting venom into an enemy, possessed by wasps and bees

Stink-bug: a member of the Pentatomidae of the order Hemiptera able to exude a noxious secretion giving off an unpleasant odour to repel enemies

Sub-social: not fully social, only partly developed along the evolutionary path to full sociality

Sub-group: a group within a larger group, whose members share certain physiological or behavioural characteristics

Sub-marginal: below the margin

Suctorial: capable of, or adapted for, sucking plant-juices or animal body-fluids through the mouthparts, usually through a tube called the proboscis

Sugaring: the process of smearing trees with a beer-and-treacle mixture to attract moths, employed by entomologists

Swarm: a group of workers and a new queen which join together to found a new wasp or bee colony

Swarming: the act of forming a swarm (q.v.)

Symbiosis: the living together of two partners, which may be both plant, both animal or animal and plant

Symbiotic: a partner in a relationship involving symbiosis; the habit of symbiosis

Symphyta: a sub-division of the Hymenoptera; the sawflies and horntails

Tabanid: a member of the family Tabanidae of the order Diptera

Tangential: built at an angle to the pillar or vertical column supporting the combs in a wasps' nest

Terminal bud: the top bud on a twig

Termites: the Isoptera

Terrestrial: living on or in the earth

Thoracic: pertaining to the thorax or chest

Thorax: the second division of the insect body, or chest, to which the wings and legs are attached

Tiger-beetle: a member of the beetle family Cicindelidae

Torpid: comatose, as during hibernation

Tree-frog: an arboreal frog, many species of which occur in tropical and sub-tropical regions

Turret: the tower-like structure found at the entrance to some mud-nesting wasps' burrows

Unisexual generation: the first of two alternating generations (q.v.) producing individuals of one sex only

Vascular channels: the channels through which water is drawn up the plant body from the roots

Vector: a carrier

Vegetarian: plant-eating

Velvet ant: the popular name for a member of the wasp family Mutillidae

Ventral: the lower or under-surface of the body

Vertical: upright

Viscera: the vital internal organs

Viviparous: bringing forth living young

Warning coloration: brilliant insect colours, spots, stripes, eyelike markings and so on serving to warn intending predators that the insect is distasteful or poisonous

Wasp-waist: the attenuated slender first abdominal segment in most wasps, giving a narrow-waisted effect

Weaver-bird: a member of the Ploceidae, a group of small birds which build large colonies of adjacent nests in the tropics

Weevil: a member of the beetle family Curculionidae

Wet season: the monsoon or rainy season in tropical areas

Wood-wasp: the horntail

Worker: a sterile non-reproductive female which assists the queen by carrying out various duties in the nest in wasp and bee communities

Index

NOTES

NOTES

NOTES

NOTES